Kiev to Lyon

Eva d'Ews Thomson

Published by Peter Thomson, 2024.

KIEV TO LYON

First edition. August 15, 2024.

ISBN: 979-8227125941

Written by Eva d'Ews Thomson.

Table of Contents

Introduction

This book is drawn from my mother's recollections of World War II. She witnessed Babi Yar, was taken as a forced labourer to Germany, managed to stay alive there (as many did not) and emerged in 1945 as a Displaced Person with a child. All the incidents recounted here are as she told me.

Dedication

I would like to take this opportunity to express my gratitude and thanks to my husband Peter, my children and grandchildren for their patience and support. To my lecture and tutor, Maureen Bettle, for reading it and her sound critique. To my tutors, Francesca Randle–Short, Oscar Flores and Daniel Martin for their encouragement. To my friends Ricardo and Celia for reading and supporting me. Finally, I want to thank my mother Galina, whose courage carried her through to let me tell this story.

One

I remember that day. It was a clear and sunny day. The sky was an intense blue. Both sides of the road were lined with large trees and the sweet smell of honey in the air was intoxicating. A gentle breeze was moving everything in a slow and dreamy motion.

Maria and I were standing beside the road, hoping and fearing our destinies were about to change. It was August 1943, on the outskirts of Magdeburg, Germany.

We were looking in silence at the horizon in the direction of the city that we had just left behind. My thoughts were flying at the speed of light as I considered the audacity of our action.

Slowly Maria moved her head, looking straight at me, and with a shaky voice she said,

"Please Gala, let's go back."

"No, we cannot! It is too late."

I looked at her pale bony face intensely. She looked older than her age and her features were intensified by a lack of sleep and proper food. As if in a mirror I could see my reflection in her eyes, as skinny and pale as she was. I smiled at her, before she responded.

"No, it is not, we could get to the factory and explain to *Herr Oberleiter* the supervisor that we missed the transport. He might help, I think he fancies you."

I shouted "Maria! Stop this nonsense! You know that I am in love with someone else and anyway why should we go back to the camp and back to the beatings? I can't take it anymore; I don't want to! It is too late now, and we must get to Berlin."

Maria hesitated before she replied in a low voice. "They may kill us."

For a while I looked at her in silence and in that one instant the horrors of the past flashed through my mind. I shook my head, pushing those memories into a dark corner of my mind. Not now! This was not a good time to confront my ghosts and Maria was waiting for an answer.

"I know this! I know! But even so I will not go back, not now. We must stop this madness and horror, not only for me but also for the others. But you may go back Maria, it is all right. I understand because I am also scared."

And I was. Every fibre of my body was tense and alert for the very real dangers that lay before us, but my determination to reach Berlin was stronger than my fears. Once I focused on something I could not let go.

Maria was wearing the same dress that she was wearing on the day we met. Minutes ago we had taken off the overalls we were wearing over our dresses and left them behind the bushes. Maria now looked annoyed: her eyebrows were furrowed, and two red spots tainted her pale cheeks. She shook her head before answering.

"Gala, don't be stupid. We made a pact never to separate, but what good does it do us if we are going to die? We are so young, and no one will listen to us."

Now her whole face was flushed, and she was breathing fast; I could see her chest going up and down. In a whisper I said.

"Someone may listen and even if they kill us, someone will remember, and will say that it was wrong. Change may come and our lives wouldn't be lost in vain. So many good people have died, women, children and men. Perhaps our time has come to die too? Who knows? What if our destiny is to survive this war to be a witness and then tell the others how it was?"

My argument sounded weak and unconvincing; Maria was staring at the road shaking her head in disbelief. Suddenly she jumped.

"Look! Look! Gala, a car's coming!"

"Yes! Yes! We'll stop this car. Smile Maria, smile," and I added quickly "Remember that my name is Helena."

A blue limousine was approaching. We raised our hands and stopped breathing for a moment that seemed an eternity. If we were scared before, now a deeper paralysing fear overcame us.

We felt sick and empty when a friendly voice spoke to us.

"Hello there! Cheer up ladies, *bitte das is schon in ordnung* Okay! It is fine — I do not bite. Where are you going?"

The driver of the blue limousine was dressed in a light gray summer jacket that I noticed immediately was immaculately clean and crease free. I guessed that he was in his early sixties, with a big friendly smile that wrinkled an intelligent face surrounded by neatly cut white hair.

"Sir! To Berlin, Sir," Maria finally answered.

The driver of the car responded "You are both lucky. I'm going to Berlin. Come, hop in."

As soon as we were both seated the car started moving. The interior of the car was luxurious; there was a faint smell of cologne and the man behind the steering wheel was obviously someone important and rich. I wondered who he was and what danger we were in? What kind of German was he? He turned his head to the right and introduced himself.

"My name is Walter von Kornburg, and I am on my way to Berlin to visit my daughter and grandson. They moved to Berlin a while ago. What are your names?"

Maria answered quickly "I am Maria, and this is my friend Gala, oh, uh! Sorry, I mean Helena."

I could have strangled Maria at that moment. Before I had time to react and think of something to save us from the situation if that was possible, Walter von Kornberg said "Gala... it sounds beautiful. I like your name. Is it Russian? Oh no! No, you could not be! So ... so you are escapees. Ha-ha! Don't be scared; I will not report you. But tell me, why to Berlin?"

The car was silent except for the humming noise of the engine.

"We must go to the *Arbeitsamt,* the labour office," Maria gasped thinly. I could see in the back mirror that von Kornberg was raising his eyebrows in an expression of surprise.

"What do you mean?" he asked.

I responded in my broken German, as I was starting to have doubts if I could trust Maria's judgement about which information was safe to disclose.

"I mean to lodge an official complaint, on.. against *Herr Commandant.* A..a.. a, he is the commander. For.. on behalf of all slave workers at the camp, I think.. no, I believe it is our right."

Darling Maria, she was such a wonderful friend and she spoke beautiful German, but I realised that her fear could put us in a greater danger. Today, sometimes I wonder where she is. Is she still alive and happy? Did she finish her degree in architecture? Did she get married and end up having the bunch of beautiful children that she dreamed of on some better nights in Gross-Ottersleben? But going back to my story; Walter now was laughing again.

"Ha! Ha! I do not believe this. It is extraordinary, ha! Ha! Ha!" Our host was shaking with laughter, his head bouncing like a balloon. I started to worry that we might have an accident but then he drove to the side of the road, put on the brake and the car stopped.

Walter slowly turned his head, his serious eyes meeting mine. In a gentle voice he said, "I believe you mean it; you really do. You must tell me more. These days we never hear about rights, morals, or justice. Yes my dear, the only justice that exists now in Germany is the Fuhrer. It may look as if all Germans are blind, but no, we are not, and some of us feel shame."

I was completely stunned by what I was hearing. I could not believe our good luck and I closed my eyes for a fraction of a second, tasting the meaning of his words. Many years later I still can feel the strong emotion of relief and hope I felt then.

After a while, I responded very slowly. "We both are working for Krupp Industry fourteen to sixteen hours a day, seven days a week with hardly any food, and on top of it the Commandant comes rushing in at any time during the night. He does so usually after hours of drinking. He beats us up randomly for no other reason than to satisfy his sadistic needs. Many of us have suffered horrendous accidents at work because of the lack of sleep and because we are too tired to concentrate properly. When someone has an accident an ambulance takes them away and we don't know what happens to them. They simply vanish, and some of us wonder where are they? Now they are talking about increasing production, but how? In these conditions, it is impossible. So, we decided that something must be done."

Walter was listening quietly and intently and when I finished, he said "You both are very brave or very naive. No don't get angry! I'm not against you. But you must know that you are putting yourselves in a very dangerous situation. The Gestapo must be searching for you."

"I don't think so. Usually the count happens at evening and only at the camp. I don't think that the supervisor will report on us, although I am not so sure about the *Herr Director* of the factory. Once or twice a week he arrives in the company of the supervisor. They both walk around, and the supervisor explains whatever is necessary. No, I don't think that he ever gets involved with the workers. He has his supervisors in every building for this," Maria responded in a very brave tone of voice.

Before he started the engine, Walter von Kornburg said "We must hope so. You both must be hungry. Gala, in the basket next to you there is some food. My house keeper made it up and she always puts too much."

Too much food! How could there be too much food? We never had too much. We always had too little food. Maria and I silently ate this banquet of bread, cheese, and apples. Since the Gestapo picked me up at my home this was the first time that I felt a bit relaxed, even if it was not for long. The rest of our trip I spent mostly in silence contemplating the passing landscape, which for most of the time was a flat land of green grass and forests. Maria and Walter were lost in their discussion about the Renaissance period. I think they talked about art, or perhaps architecture. Maria once told me that when the war started she was a first-year student at Warsaw University and that she was studying architecture. Maria was always talking about styles and designs. Meanwhile I was dreaming that I was home in the dining room with my family. My brother Anatoly would tell us a funny story and we all would laugh; the stories that Anatoly told were always funny.

Suddenly I came back to reality remembering the purpose of our trip and started to shiver again, asking myself what was waiting for us in Berlin? I tried to imagine what we were going to do once we got there. We would be in a foreign city, and not know where the *Arbeitsamt* was. Just as I was about to ask Walter if he had any idea where we had to go, Maria asked him?

"Do you know where the *Arbeitsamt* is?"

"No, I do not know," responded Walter and added, "But my daughter, she may know as she works in the *Armament Ministerium* as a secretary, so she must know. Not that she needs to work; it would be better if she stayed home and took care of her child. But never mind this - she will know where the *Arbeitsamt* is."

He went silent after he said this and for the rest of the trip no one spoke. After the last bend of the road we had our first glimpses of the city of Berlin. At first it looked like some grey and white spots in the distance but as we drove near, buildings took shape and soon we were driving between large grey buildings. Some of the buildings were built in the baroque and some in the gothic style.

We approached the centre of the city and the architecture became more imposing. It was obvious that it meant to impress. And possibly it did. Maria and I both had lived in big cities and were used to big buildings.

This was still very impressive, and we felt intimidated by all the movement on the streets. Armed soldiers were guarding the entrances of lots of the buildings. Walter stopped the car in front of a very large grey building. It was occupying an entire block with two armed soldiers guarding the very large entry.

"Here we are," said Walter, turning his head towards us. "I will go and see my daughter and find out where you must go. Please stay in the car — you are safer here and I will not be long."

Walter left us and went towards the entrance. I could see the soldiers saluting him and then he disappeared through the large carved door. Maria and I sat silent. Though fear never left us since the war began, we had stopped thinking about it for a while, driving along the country road and reassured by Walter's friendliness. But now it hit back at us with all its might.

"Gala, what do you think will happen next?" Maria asked in a shaky voice.

"I do not know. Let's wait and see," I responded.

Shortly after we saw Walter coming out of the building. He approached the car quickly, opened the door and said "You both are very lucky, because you both work in an ammunition factory that is under the umbrella of this Ministry. Hop out! I will come in with you to the office where you must go, but afterwards, I am afraid, I must go."

Before we approached the big doors he added "I had great pleasure in meeting both of you and I wish you the best of luck."

"Heil Hitler!" the two soldiers who were guarding the big doors shouted.

"Yes, *heil!" r*esponded Walter von Kornburg with a gesture of impatience and we entered the building. What a sight! Big white marble stairs wound up in the middle of a big hall and people were rushing in and out through many doors. We climbed the stairs to the next floor where two huge German banners with swastikas hung on the wall in front of us. We passed them to the left and continued walking for a while along long corridors, until we stopped in front of a carved double winged door, clearly the office of an important person. The other doors were less elaborate.

Walter knocked on the door, and a man's voice responded.

"Herein! Yes, please come in."

The man who was sitting behind the large antique desk was middle aged and looking glum. He was fat and with a red blotched face, and his coal-black eyes were looking puzzled as he looked at us. He was wearing a military uniform; I do not know what exactly his rank was, but he must be at least a major or a colonel. His name was Brand; Walter called him that before he introduced himself.

"Baron von Kornburg."

The two men shook hands, and Walter introduced us.

"These two young ladies are here to make a complaint against their Commandant."

Brand looked us in surprise and moved his head from me to Maria and then very slowly he asked "Explain please."

We started to explain about the beatings, lack of food, sleepless nights and how it affected our work and production. Most of the time he seemed quite bored with my accounts of the bad treatment and only when I mentioned production did he seem to revive and become very interested. After I finished my account and went silent, he looked at me sternly for a while.

"You can go! I will take care of this," he assured Walter. "I will see what I can do and do not worry, they will be fine. I give you my word of honour."

Walter turned to us and said very slowly but loud enough so Brand could hear him.

"Do not worry! You are in good hands, and I will visit you at the factory in Magdeburg. You can tell me then how it all went."

He saluted Brand with a quick *Heil Hitler!* and left the room. I regretted that he had to leave. Somehow, he reminded me of my father, and I felt safe with him. Again, we felt lost and afraid in this large room, with its walls painted white. There were two French-style windows on the left side of the room with long dark blue velvet curtains hanging on both sides of the windows. Large red Persian carpets covered in part a beautifully designed parquet floor, and two big armchairs were standing in front of this big antique oak desk. On the wall behind the desk Hitler's portrait was hanging, a big photograph in black and white. The opposite wall was partially covered with a big copy of a painting: Napoleon and his army at Waterloo. On the right wall hung a portrait of Frederick the Great and two smaller paintings of an alpine view. This room was ostentatious and clearly intended to impress. Brand was talking to someone on the phone. I could not understand as he spoke very quickly and sounded very impatient, saying lots of '*Ja, ja, das ist schon in ordnung*'. Later Maria told me that he rang somebody and discussed production. Apparently he had thought for some time that something was wrong in the Krupp factory in Magdeburg. Production was low but he did not know why. He had had previous complaints but nothing concrete. Now he had the answer to the problem. The Commandant, he was the culprit, and it could easily be fixed.

"We need soldiers on the eastern front, do we not?" he asked foxily. "We will replace the incompetent man with someone who has a better vision of the national need. What did you say? Oh that! Yes, you are right and yes, they are pretty! Oh, you are very fast, yes you are! Ha! Ha! Ha! Ha! Ha-a! Ha-a-a-a-a-!"

He was bending with laughter. We both stood there silent and tense. That we both were afraid was a gentle way to say we were terrified. This frightful fear would overcome us, again and again. We felt always extremely vulnerable and never felt completely safe, not until the war ended. Maria stood next to me in silence. I hardly could hear her breathing but then Brand put down the phone and rubbing his small fat hands together, he smiled. He really did! Then he gestured us to sit down on the big armchairs that stood in front of his desk. Just in time! My fear made me feel quite dizzy and I was afraid that I might faint. Brand must have noticed our fear, and therefore he reached for a bottle of brandy, which together with half a dozen glasses was standing on a tray on the top of his desk.

He filled three glasses and he passed one glass to me and other to Maria, offering us a drink.

"Please, drink. It is fine, it is imported from France, drink, please drink," he insisted laughingly. I nearly choked; never had I drunk alcohol and it was so strong. Soon I started to feel dizzy, but this time I think it was the effect of the alcohol. Maria had tears in her eyes but very bravely she continued to drink. Brand was laughing and he shouted out "It is strong! It is very good! It is French! *Gesundheit.*"

There was a knock on the door and two young soldiers in uniform arrived.

"Heil Hitler!" they saluted quickly.

"Heil Hitler!" responded Brand and whispered something to them. They looked at us sideways in surprise and, after some debate and lots of head nodding, they came to stand beside us and Brand said.

"Go with them. They will drive you back to Magdeburg, and everything is taken care of. Do not worry, go!"

I thanked him, not knowing exactly why, but it seemed polite. The soldiers saluted again *Heil Hitler! a*nd Brand responded *Heil Hitler!*

The four of us went outside to the courtyard at the back of the building. There was a grey car with its engine running, waiting. One other soldier was waiting in the driver's seat. The soldiers told us to sit in the back seats, together with one of the soldiers; the other sat next to the driver. Our trip back to Gross-Ottersleben we spent mostly in silence, very worried about what was waiting for us. I dreaded to think what the Commandant would do to us. What form of punishment would he give us? Yes, those were very uncertain times. Once we were interrupted from our thoughts when the soldier that was sitting next to me offered us cigarettes.

"Please, have a cigarette. What is your name?"

"Thank you, but we are non-smokers. My name is Gala, and this is my friend Maria." I answered quickly and went silent again. I must confess that he was a very good-looking man and so were the other two soldiers. He was smiling at me in a friendly way and before he pulled an apple from the pocket of his jacket he introduced himself as Karl.

He then cut the apple in half with a pocketknife and passed the halves to Maria and me. In other times and in different circumstances we could have talked more to them. We all were around the same age and probably would have had lots of questions and things of interest to talk about. But this was wartime, and I could never forget that they were the invaders of my country. I couldn't forget what their compatriots did to my friend Pola and her family and why I was in this place, far away from my own family. No, I could not forget. Therefore, I stayed silent.

Two

"Come on! Gala! Hurry up. We will be late."

"Do not worry, Pola. We have only our music lesson for the first hour and Irina Petrovna is always late. I don't think that today it will be different."

Klac! Klac! Klac! was the sound of boots on the street, wet after last night's heavy rain. Marching soldiers of the Reich dressed in grey uniforms and black shining boots. The citizens of Kiev were standing on the side of the road watching the soldiers marching in lines of five. They looked magnificent, good looking, holding their backs straight and with eyes that were looking forward, showing strong purpose. I was not afraid; on the contrary, I felt an inexplicable exaltation that was accompanied by a pleasant shiver. Unexpectedly I noticed that one of the soldiers winked an eye at me and he smiled, showing his magnificent teeth.

I turned my head and said excitedly to Pola "Did you see! Did you see that! Did you see how that soldier smiled at me, and he.."

I went silent as Pola was looking at me seriously and I noticed a tinge of sadness in her voice.

"Oh, Gala! Don't you realise that no matter how good looking they are, they are the invaders and our enemy. Remember that our fathers still have memories of the last war."

She said it in a low voice, nearly whispering, and no one could have heard her. I lowered my head as I couldn't support the intensity of her eyes and could feel the heat rising to my head. I could feel my cheeks going red. I was ashamed that I showed so little tact and dignity in front of my friend, but also I felt embarrassed that someone could have heard her.

"Yes! Let's go to school! You are right, Pola: we are going to be late."

I held Pola's arm and quickly we left the crowd in the direction of our school. We walked in silence. I was split in two; on one hand I was agreeing with my friend, but on other I was calling her envious, silly and conservative. Which was not true, but I needed a justification? How otherwise could I explain my loss of control? Blaming my friend made me fill less responsible for my reaction.

As we approached the school, I realised that now I would have to justify our lateness to Irina Petrovna. As we got to the corner we saw something, and Pola instinctively pushed me back against the wall. Hidden behind the wall we could observe movement at the entrance to our school. A grey truck was standing there with some German soldiers standing in front. They were smoking and laughing. As we were considering what to do the school's main door opened and Irina Petrovna stepped out with her arms held over her head, followed by Michael Ivanovich, our history teacher. He too, was holding his arms up and four heavily armed German soldiers were pushing them forward to the truck. Quickly they got into the truck and immediately it started moving and some instants later they disappeared from our sight.

Hesitant, we started walking across the road when other students appeared from inside the building. Some were excited, screaming that today there were no classes, others were crying, but the majority were in silence. I took Pola's hand, squeezing it hard as I suddenly realised that from today our lives would not be the same. I looked up the sky that seemed to be the same, grey and cloudy, but something had changed. There was an inexplicable apprehension in the air. We all started to leave, hurrying home and here too I had a surprise. As soon I opened the door my father told me that my three brothers had gone across the Dnieper without saying goodbye.

"They left to fight the enemy," said my father.

This was the second time today that I heard the word enemy. The word started to take the form of the good-looking smiling soldier who winked at me. How could it be? That these beautiful people were our enemies? No, it wasn't possible, surely it was a mistake.

A few days later my universe collapsed. Accelerated events shifted it millions of degrees in another direction. Since then, my life was never the same. Activities at school were irregular, Nina Petrovna and Michael Ivanovich did not return, and someone brought the news that both were shot by the Germans. We all were scared about this news and other stories that would arrive at school. Other students would bring those; some were so disturbing that it was difficult to believe that they could be true. At home no one spoke about the war; those days no one spoke much, and everyone was very busy. Whenever I could, after school I would retreat to my room and in the solitude of my room I would watch the clouds through the window and let myself go in daydreams. I would dream about the good-looking enemy who would appear in the window riding a white horse with long golden crest. The soldier now was a smiling prince and as soon I went to open the window he disappeared and dissolved into the clouds. Some days later there was a spectacular sunrise. Everything was shining bright and clear. The air was cold, and it felt that the winter was not far away.

My friend Pola dropped by the early afternoon and convinced me to go for a stroll in the forest. I accepted happily; we didn't have a lot to do in those days and I always had a good time with Pola. She was more than a friend; she was my adviser and I loved her as if she was my sister. She was intelligent, read lots, and there was not a subject that I could not talk about with her. But the best was her sense of humour and she always made me laugh.

Returning from this long walk in the forest, on such a beautiful autumn day, the air was crisp, and the sun was setting slowly.

It was illuminating everything in an orange reddish colour, and we were feeling invigorated. The last thing we needed was a confrontation with Nina who sometimes was very confronting, although not without love! I knew that she loved me very much, but she was overly protective.

"Gala! Hurry up! Galina!" she screamed rudely.

"Gala, please answer her. Otherwise she will wake the entire neighbourhood," Pola said, bursting with laughter.

"I know, Pola, but my sister can drive me crazy. Since our mother's death she has tried to take her role. As if someone ever asked her to. She is only one year older than me; Nina would never call the boys like this," I responded, hanging my head and letting my mind wander far away, trying to imagine where my brothers were. Pola asking about them brought me back to reality.

"And how are your good-looking brothers, Gala?"

"I don't know Pola; we haven't heard from them for a while. I assume that they are well in Moscow, I miss them."

I went silent, thinking about my three brothers who left to join the Red Army on the same day that the Germans marched into Kiev. We had not heard from them since. I was worried about them, but also was hoping that they were still alive and fine and that they had managed to join the Red Army and were fighting the Germans. We came up to Nina who looked awful; she was pale, and her eyes were red and swollen, as if she had been crying.

My stomach twisted with pain and a dreadful thought invaded my brain. Had something had happened to my brothers?

Nina started asking "Gala, what's the matter with you? Why did you not answer, and where have you been? Father wants you home; it's getting late. You too, Pola, should go home. These are dangerous times."

"We know, we know, Nina, but sometimes it feels good to forget and pretend that everything is fine. We went to the forest looking for berries but did not find any. Sorry if we are late, it is my fault. Don't be angry with Gala."

Pola was trying to appease Nina and failed to notice how upset she was. Nina did not look her usual self and gasped as if she could not breathe.

"Nina! What is the matter with you?" I asked quietly.

She must have noticed that instead of my usual defensive tone, where I would try to avoid answering any of her questions, I was unusually quiet, and she also responded quietly.

"It is alright, I didn't want to be so abrupt, but I am upset. My God! How shall I tell you, Pola?"

Pola only now noticed how pale Nina was and she started shaking her by the shoulders. "Tell me what? Nina! What's wrong, why are you so pale? Oh my God! Something has happened to my family! Nina talk to me! Please say something."

Pola was screaming now. Nina went silent for a moment and then she started crying and muttered slowly between sobs.

"At first, I thought that you were with them, but then Dad told me that you and Gala went for a walk, but surely you must have read the posters this morning. It ordered that all Jews must go to Babi Yar, for resettlement."

I remembered then what we had read that this morning. The poster was glued to the school door when we passed it on our way to the forest. We thought that it was a very strange request but the warm sun on a September day and the autumnal colours of the beautiful forest put a spell on us, and we forgot all about it. Now that Nina mentioned it the whole weight of this notice struck me like lightning. Pola was continuing screaming at Nina.

"For God's sake! Nina! Stop this! Tell me what happened to my family? Tell me now! Do you hear me? Now!"

Nina was shuddering now; I could hear her teeth chattering. Nina grabbed Pola's hands, before she whispered.

They took them! The Germans took them! Oh Pola! I am so sorry, but where are you going? Pola! Gala! Come back!"

As soon as Nina said that Pola's family had been taken away, Pola started running in the direction of Babi Yar and of course I was not going to leave her alone.

"Just stop running both of you. You will draw attention, and that is the last thing you need now. Please think.. calm down and think," Nina was saying in a pleading voice.

"Pola, Nina is right. We would do better if we calmed down and started deciding what to do," I pointed out to her, and Pola slowed her pace before saying

"But Gala, why would they take them to the forest and not to the train station? It would make more sense. I have such a horrible stomach ache. I feel sick ... I dread to think what may happen. I must go and find out."

I took her hand and squeezed it and I said firmly "I understand, Pola. I am coming too."

Nina was running behind us. She got hold of the sleeves of our coats and forced us to stop at the same time as she was shouting at me "No, you are not! You are going home with me, and now! Did you hear me, Gala?"

Gently I opened Nina's hands that were holding my coat and freed myself from her.

"Yes, Nina I did, I did hear you. Go home and tell Daddy that I could not leave my friend. He will understand."

Nina started crying and she was now begging, pleading, dropping her air of control. "*Galinka maia*, please came with me, don't do this to me, please, I love you! I am scared for you."

How dear she was to me in this moment. I hesitated for a second over whether I was doing the right thing. But then I decided that the only thing I could do was to stay with Pola – she had only me. I looked into Nina's teary eyes and said very slowly.

"I love you too, Nina, and very much. Be good and go home to Daddy. I will be fine, I will take care of both of us, I promise. Go now. Go."

"You know, she is right. You should go with her," Pola said. She was looking at Nina's back shaken by sobs as she slowly started her way home. Then she looked at me and added.

"This has nothing to do with you, Gala. You are not a Jew."

"And you don't look like one," I answered quickly and put my arm under Pola's. Pola was blonde with big blue eyes, a small nose and full lips in a beautifully shaped face. She looked more French to me. Not that I knew many French people then, but I remember seeing some French movies and the women in these movies looked like Pola.

"Even so, it doesn't change the fact that I am," said Pola.

"Fine, Pola! Promise me one thing. No matter what is happening you will stay with me. We will stay behind and watch. And then we decide what to do? Promise," I insisted, worrying. I did not know what exactly was awaiting us but had a bad feeling. What happened was beyond my imagination.

"All right, I promise, I promise," Pola answered.

As we approached Babi Yar, there was a strange vibration in the air, and everything was moving in slow motion. Heavy silence surrounded us; a thin mist was coming from the riverside down in the forest. Then we heard it, a gunshot.

"Be quiet Pola, we are almost there. Posh, posh, did you hear that?"

"What was that? Oh no! They are shooting," gasped Pola.

"Hold my hand. Let's go from this side. Can you see those big trees with shrubs under them? We will hide there. I think we will be able to see what is happening."

I grabbed Pola's hand and pulled her down. We advanced slowly between the trees, silently and bent over on all fours, and then we saw it. For the rest of my life, I will not forget the scene that played out in front of my eyes. Old men, women, children, old people and very young, babies in their mothers, arms, all naked, standing in front of a very long trench dug recently. They all were very silent, even the children. The German were sending small groups of people to run on the wooden planks, which were placed over the ravine.

Then as they ran, they were shooting them and their lifeless bodies would fall into the overfilled grave dug on the bottom of the ravine and ... no, I could never forget. Never! Pola, next to me, was trembling and I could hear the rattle of her teeth and then in a shaky voice she cried out,

"Oh! My God! Oh, look there is mum, my sister! Daddy! Oh! My God! Oh! My God! They are killing them!"

I pulled Pola into my arms and put my hand across her mouth. I feared that if we were discovered they would shoot us too.

"Hold to me Pola and be quiet darling, quiet. Cry, cry, but be silent! Hold on to me, hold me!" I was trembling myself and was holding on to Pola who was shaking, not only to give her some warmth and comfort, but to for myself as well.

"Gala, I am so cold," Pola was whispering, looking at me with ghostly eyes. She haunted and lost. I looked again, trying to convince myself that this was only a bad dream from which we would soon wake up and find that nothing had happened.

Then I saw him, my beautiful enemy and invader, without his white horse: there he was smiling, looking at the killing and showing off his perfect white teeth. In his hand he was holding a burning cigarette that he carelessly threw into the ravine. So good looking and...I saw that as he moved his form started to change. And a metamorphosis happened, and the change was horrible. His face got a dark grayish color, long hair was growing out of his nose, his lips were large, and he was missing some teeth, he looked grotesque. I felt desperation and pain for Pola's family shot dead but also for the loss of my beautiful enemy. We could not move from where we were without running the risk of discovery. In my desperation and crazy as it may sound, I started telling Pola children's stories to escape from the orgy and madness of the killings that had taken place in front of us. We must have fallen asleep from exhausting when a sadden noise woke us up. Someone with a wheezing voice was saying in Ukrainian to someone else.

"Nearly missed him ha, ha, ha."

I heard other voice responding with laughter -ha, ha..., then it went silent. I was shivering from cold and from fear; every so often we heard gunshots. But we stopped looking in front of us, and I started telling Pola another children's story.

"There was once a little princess who wanted to fly and this horrible witch always tried to stop her, but one day a good, nice Prince arrived and.. come on Pola, let's go back, it is getting dark again, the Germans have left, come Pola lets go home. We can do nothing here; they are all dead!"

"My family! O*h! Elohim Adonai!* Where shall I go? I don't have where to go any more; I do not have a home. They destroyed everything that was dear to me. I may as well die. I feel like it would be better if they have had killed me too," Pola cried. I was holding her hand as we started walking towards the city when I stopped. My foot hit something soft, and I looked down to discover the naked body of a small child, no more than three years old. He must have been the child that those two men were laughing at and talking about. Poor little darling, he tried to run away but did not manage it. A small red spot just above his ear showed where the bullet went in.

This lifeless child was lying only thirty meters from where we were hiding. It was a wonder that those men did not discover us. I broke a branch from a tree and covered the little body. Pola said a prayer and to my relief, Pola started to cry.

Sobbingly she was saying "I want to die too, please, dear God, take me."

"No, you must live," I interrupted her. "You must avenge them."

"But, but how?" Pola was whispering, she looked pale and fragile.

"You remember Kola Wojciech? He was in our class, and he told me that he was going to join the Red Army. Next day he disappeared, and this happened two days ago. Be at the railway bridge, between three o'clock and dawn. You must wear a green scarf. Someone will come and take you across. This is what he told me."

I took hold of Pola's hand and was urging her to hurry up. It was getting late, and we had to be very careful and quiet because of the curfew. We were approaching my house. Dead silence and darkness surrounded the streets, but we had to worry not only about being discovered by the Germans but also by our Ukrainian neighbour. Some of them were eager to give information to the Germans for some small privileges.

After a while Pola said "I do not know. At this moment I'm so sick, I feel like vomiting, and ..."

She started vomiting as we approached the entrance to my house. I waited for her to finish, looking away. When I looked she was very pale and cold sweat was covering her fringe. I put my arm around her shoulder; the acid small of vomit made me feel nauseous but I overcame the sickening feeling and guided her inside our apartment which was on the third floor.

"We're here, come on, let's go in."

The apartment was silent. Slowly we crossed the corridor and went into the living room. The samovar was on top of the round table in the corner, near the window and the bubbling noise of boiling water greeted us. My father was standing next to it with a grim expression on his face, looking through the windows into the darkness. He was an impressive figure, very tall with broad shoulders. Though middle-aged, he still had a slim waist.

I adored my father and I think that all five of us kids loved and respected him immensely. Our heavily pregnant mother had died during the Holodomor (Stalin's famine) from hunger. For the past ten years our father had brought us up with love. It must have been very hard for him, for he was still young and in need of companionship, but he always put us kids first. There was hardly anything that he would not do for us.

My older brother Anatoly once told me that dad emigrated to America and settled in Boston. Apparently in Boston he started a relation with an American woman who became mother of his two boys. When his father died, he came over to help his brother and mother to take care of the family property. Two days after his arrival the First World War started, he was arrested, and his passport was confiscated. His brother died on the Austrian Front. He had to take care of his ailing mother and the property. Then in 1917 the first Revolution happened, and he met my mother, who was much younger than he. They fell deeply in love and married. Maybe, because he had lost one family and knew the pain of losing love, our family became more precious to him. Whatever the reasons, to me he was and is a wonderful father.

He looked at Pola and me, his eyes softened and a big smile appeared which wrinkled his handsome face. He opened his arms, and I ran towards him, ran into his arms and felt safe at last.

"Hello Daddy! Nina! I'm sorry that I am late, but something very horrible happened," I started saying in a shaky voice, but he interrupted me.

"We know, we know! Pola come here, give me a hug. Poor thing, you are shivering. Cry, and cry little pigeons, cry! Hopefully tears and time will help to ease some of your pain."

Our bodies were shaking from crying. Now that we didn't have to worry about being discovered and in the safety of my home, we unwound and relived the horror of the past day. My father was holding us in silence and protectively until we calmed down. Then he started talking again.

"Nina told me. I went to the market and people were talking about it. What a horror. We must leave tomorrow. It is time for me to join the army. You, Gala, and you, Nina, will travel to Moscow. You both will stay with Aunty Musia. Have something to eat and go to bed. You must have some sleep. We will go early in the morning."

He bent and took a bundle from one of the chairs, which he pushed towards Pola, saying at the same time "Pola, you must go now. Here grab this bundle with some bread and spare clothing. Nina put it together for you; I will take you across the river. This is the best I can do."

Pola nodded in silence and then she said in between sobs "Thank you, Gregory Troyansky, thank you. I know that I am putting all of you in great danger. Goodbye Nina, goodbye *daragaya Galinka,* my dear friend, I will always remember you, and miss you."

I ran towards my friend, realising that I might never see her again. "Pola give me a hug! Please be very careful, take care of yourself. Remember always that you must avenge your family and the others remember! You must stay alive! I love you and I will miss you too. Promise that you will write, whenever it's possible. So will I and stop crying! Do not cry ever again! Not until you have had your revenge, do you hear me Pola? Go now. Good luck. And go, go now, go."

Daddy and Pola left and again there was a heavy silence only interrupted by the noise of bubbling water. Nina went to the table, and filled two cups with strong tea to which she added lots of sugar and then passed one cup to me. There is nothing more comforting than a cup of strong, sweet tea. I looked at my sister and asked

"Nina, do you think they will be okay? I did not know that Daddy was the person who was taking people to the other side."

"Me neither."

Nina crossed the room to sit on the sofa. She looked her old self now; her hair was combed tidily away from her fringe and she was wearing a clean woollen dress. She was not as tall as me, but she had a slim and elegant figure.

"Nina, I am so scared. You don't know how very scared I am. There in the forest I thought I will never see you or Daddy again. Do you think we will be safe with Aunty Musia? She might not want us, and anyway she is not a real aunty."

"Do not worry about it now, Gala. First we must get there. I remember her. She visited us once when Mum was still alive. She is our cousin and I remember that she was nice."

Nina smiled at me with reassurance and slowly I started sipping my tea, lost in my thoughts about the events of the past hours and what they meant. What kind of consequence would this have on Pola or our life? This was when I heard the noise of cars stopping, I jumped to my feet and went to the window.

"Did you hear that? It sounded like the brakes of a car," I asked Nina before opening the window to look outside.

"What are you doing Gala? Close the window! Come and sit here, next to me," Nina called out.

"Nina, the Gestapo is here! They have come for us! Someone must have betrayed us! There is nowhere we can go now; this is the end," I cried.

"Gala, come, sit next to me and hold my hand," Nina said calmly. "They are at the door! They are knocking! Give me a kiss and stop crying, as you told Pola to do. Stop now! We do not have much time. No matter what and no matter where we are or when, do not forget this address, Gala! We will meet here again. God bless you."

I fell into Nina's comforting arms and whispered "Look, look, I am not crying. I will be brave no matter what.

"Los aufschlissen! Los! Los! Aufmachen! Oder we werden schissen!" I was holding Nina tightly; we heard a single shot and within seconds some twenty heavily armed German soldiers were in the room. Five of them surrounded us, the others were running through the flat destroying things on their way. They shot at the doors in every room before going in, at the cupboards before opening them as if we were hiding the Red Army in them. Then an official came and stood in front of us, asking lots of questions. Our neighbour from downstairs, Mr. Korolev, was there and he was translating what the German was saying. They asked us about Pola and where she was? Nina said that she had no idea where or what? Korolev hit her across her face, and he was screaming at her.

"Liar! You are a liar! I saw her coming upstairs with Gala. Where are you hiding her? And where is your father anyway?"

Nina was bleeding from lips that were swelling fast, as was her cheek. She must have been in lots of pain, but she stayed silent and looked Korolev straight in his eyes. I was quiet but my mind was spinning very fast. Where was father and did he and Pola manage to cross the Dnieper River? Are they safe? What will happen to us? Finely Korolev turned his head to the side and the German official said something that Korolev had to translate again.

"Go and follow those soldiers down to the car."

Before we left the flat, I grabbed our coats that were hanging in the corridor on a hook nailed on to the wall. Outside was dark and very cold. Except us and the Germans I couldn't see a soul. Before I got into the car, I looked for the last time up at the windows of our flat and I could see some of our neighbours looking down through the windows. The entire neighbourhood looked solemn and serious and probably also scared. The car drew away and we were taken to the train station. The soldiers signalled us to follow them, and we arrived at a platform where a goods train was standing. The train was loaded with people, old, young, and children all squeezing in the small windows, many crying. They all had the same hunted look. This hunted look was constantly present during the war. Nina and I were told to climb into one of the wagons.

Three

"Oops! Sorry, but it is very squashy here." A good-looking young brunette smilingly pushed me gently.

"It's all right; come, squeeze in here next to the window; you will find more air to breathe and can see out a bit," I responded, smiling back at her. Nina and I had been travelling since the Germans took us away from our home in Kiev. We had been in this overcrowded goods wagon for many weeks. The train would stop in different locations for hours and sometimes for days. Our wagon smelt of human sweat and urine. The constant cries of the weak due to hunger and dehydration were nerve wracking and we were hungry. The Germans sometimes threw some stale bread into the wagon on one of the stops. This time the train stopped in a large city. We had arrived in Warsaw, and they loaded the overcrowded wagons with more people. We stayed there for over two weeks. The young women that joined us had a pleasant voice and she spoke good Russian, as well as Polish and German and, as I found out later, she also knew French.

"This is good. We will know where we are going. By the way, my name is Leah."

"Oh! Oh! You meant Maria, no?" I asked her with an unsteady voice. But she insisted she was called by her real name.

"No, I meant Leah!"

"I heard you, but from now on, it will be better if you forget this name. Start calling yourself Maria and it may save your life. I am Gala and I like you. You are the first person smiling since we left home. This is my sister Nina. Nina this is Maria, she is coming with us, and she speaks Russian."

The bundle on the floor that was my sister stirred, a hollow face with two big blue eyes popped out of the bundle, and in a squeaky voice Nina said "And where to? You sound as if we are on some holiday trip, and we are not! Wake up to yourself Gala!"

There were times that I hated my sister, and this was one. I was trying very hard to ignore reality and she insisted on being very realistic. I needed to escape into the sphere between reality and fantasy. Most of the time I could clearly distinguish between both zones, but sometimes I was trapped there in between and refused to leave, because it felt safe.

"It is all right, Nina. I know that we are not in an ideal situation, but we may as well do the best we can. Being angry and gloomy all the time will not make any difference to what happens to us. We may as well have some fun if we can."

Leah looked at me still smiling and said "Gala, you are so very right. I feel that when I smile everybody gets disoriented, even the Germans. They get less tense and pushy with me."

"Yes, I think that is a good tactic. I will try to smile more myself, but I must admit it may be difficult to smile at the Germans. I will never forget what they did back home."

"Tell me Gala, why did you insist that I change my name. What difference does it make?"

"Because Leah is a Jewish name, no? And after what the Germans did to my friend's family? I will tell you, but I must warn you it is a very disturbing story. Come a bit nearer." As gently as it was possible and in very quiet voice I told Leah about Babi Yar, about Pola and the killing of her family.

Leah was listening quietly and then she cried out "Oh Gala! This cannot be true? But on the other hand I heard that here in Poland, the German did some horrible things to Jews. Shortly after the invasion I was staying with friends, on their property in the country, next to Ciechanow. My friends and I were attending the same faculty in Warsaw. My father was professor at the university, and they knew each other. One night they arrived home and told us that the Germans were going to move all the Jews into the Ghetto. After dinner they went to my father's studio and what was discussed, I do not know, but when they all came out my father told me to pack some of my belongings and that I was going to stay for a while with my friends in the country. I was living happily on their property until one week ago. This is when the Gestapo arrived to pick me up. Since then, I've been travelling, first by car, then in a truck and now in this train. I do not know where my family is or what happened to them? I have a brother and a sister, and they are younger than me."

Before responding I took Leah into my arms, in an urge to comfort and to protect her.

"They may be fine... Let's hope so. What else can you do?" I added and Leah went silent for a while. Then she said firmly, "I think that you are right; I shall from now on be called Maria Bogdanowska."

"Bogdanowska", I asked in surprise.

"Yes, Bogdanowska. This is the name of my Polish friends in Ciechanow, and they are not Jews."

"This is good, Maria Bogdanowska," I answered my new friend and we both started laughing.

"Why are you both giggling? What's so funny?" Nina asked, shaking her head.

"Nothing Nina, nothing, do not worry. Maria just told me something funny."

Nina was looking at us quietly. Poor thing, she looked pale, and I was seriously worried about her health. I knew that she was not well, though she tried to hide it from me. I noticed that she was sweating during the nights when asleep and sometime, she would cough. Now she was shaking her head in disbelief and added slowly before disappearing into her bundle again.

"I do not know how you do this Gala, but sometimes I think you don't care what is happening to us."

"Nina, I do care, but what can we do now? Jump from the train? I told you we should jump there in Ukraine, but you said that it was a silly idea."

"And it was! We could have died under the train!"

We possibly could have gone on like this for a while, but Maria intervened.

"Why don't you both stop fighting and we can have some sleep. I am very tired; I have not slept since I left my friend's house."

"We are not fighting, but Nina is very nervous since we left home. She is worried and does not sleep well. You are right, we should have some sleep. Good night!" I responded with a yawn. Shortly after I was deeply asleep and having very strange dreams about Pola, but Pola was not Pola, it was Maria.

Then I dreamt about Mum, and she was alive, so sweet. She walked toward me with her big smile and in her hands, she was holding red poppy flowers. I didn't want to wake up, but no one could resist Nina for very long.

"Hey! Wake up! Maria! Gala! The train has stopped! We have arrived, I think."

We jumped to our feet and squeezed our faces to the window bars. We could see lines of dirty wooden barracks, surrounded by a wire fence. No trees or any other vegetation was in sight; it was such a desolate place. I started to feel sweat dribbling down my spine although it was a cold morning.

"Where are we?" I asked in fear and cried out "Look Maria! Nina look! Look at those barracks and look how thin those people are! Oh! Look at that big wire fence!"

Then I turned in the direction of the exit, when I saw "Oh no! Look! They are all naked! Do they make us take our clothes off?"

I remembered Babi Yar, and the naked bodies of Pola's family and the others. A frightful fear overcame me.

"Why? Where are we?" I started asking.

"Come Gala, Nina, we better get moving," said Maria and she started walking.

The wagon doors were open and slowly it started to empty. As we walked towards the opening, I noticed some women in strange positions on the wagon floor. At first, I thought they were sleeping, but then I realised that they were not sleeping but they were dead. They possibly died from hunger, thirst or suffocation. No one knew why. And I don't think anyone would have tried to find out.

As soon as we stepped out from the wagon we saw a woman in a uniform with a letter 'K' printed on her left breast who was standing under a big sign. It was mounted on two metal posts and had a writing that said *Dachau.*

"Look, it says Dachau, Maria. Do you know where we are?"

"I think that we are in Germany. God! This place looks gloomy - and this horrible stench! Please Gala, stay with me, and you too, Nina. I am frightened. This doesn't look good!"

The women in the uniform pointed at us and started shouting "*Los! Bitte ihre kleider of, der doctor wile sie untersuchen.* Let's go! Quick, take your clothes off for the doctor's checkup."

Nina and Maria started to undress but I was still hesitating. I felt so embarrassed and frightened, but then I looked at Nina and Maria. They both stood there, with their beautiful bodies and their heads up, looking extremely proud and determined. The sun was caressing their bodies with a shimmer of gold. They looked to me like the statues of goddesses out of the Greek mythology... slowly I started to undress. The woman in the uniform was screaming. She looked impatient and was pointing to a table behind which various officers were sitting. They were wearing white open jackets over their uniforms.

We approached the table and I was looking into grey, cold eyes in a beautiful face. I was feeling cold and scared, but I was smiling; determined not to show my fear to those people who had invaded my country, stolen my youth and split my beloved family apart. No, I was very determined to stay brave no matter what happened to me. And then this strange and beautiful face was asking me?

"What is your name?"

"Gala, Gala Troyansky," I answered proudly.

"Russian?" he asked.

"No, I am from Ukraine," I responded quickly.

"How old are you?"

"Nineteen."

Then he turned to Maria and asked "And what is your name?"

"I am Maria Bogdanowska."

"Are you Polish?" he asked.

"Yes! I am," Maria answered in a firm voice.

"How old are you?"

"I am eighteen years old."

He looked us with his cold eyes, and I felt them move over my body. It was as if he was touching my body with his mind. I felt my skin getting goose bumps, my nipples stiffened and a cold sweat between my breasts and my thighs started rolling slowly down my body. I do not know how long we stood there exposed to this young doctor's scrutiny but finally he said "*In ordnung,* get dressed and go to the left."

"Take them to the trucks," he told an old soldier who was standing by, armed with a machine gun. Then he dismissed us and was looking now at another woman behind us. Somehow we managed to get dressed and were walking in the direction of the trucks. Maria was holding my arm so as to give support to her and me.

I breathed deeply before I said to my friend "Maria, I am so glad we are together, but where is Nina?"

I noticed then the two soldiers that were taking my sister away. I tried to run towards her, but Maria firmly held my arms.

"Nina! Nina! Nina! Nina-a," I screamed in her direction. 'Nina!"

Nina turned her head quickly and cried out "Gala! Galinka! Maria! Please, take care of her!"

Maria now was talking firmly and urgently to me. "Do not cry Galina, she will be fine; they are taking her also to the trucks. Smile for now, smile and hurry up, the quicker we get into this truck the better."

Everything was happening so fast; I did not have time to recover from one shock and I was in for another one. I felt exhausted, but so was Maria. I tried to put on a brave face, but inside I felt sick. My stomach was aching, and it was more than just hunger.

"Yes, I think you are right, there is nothing we can do for now. But tell me Maria; what is it saying on this card that they gave us?"

"It says that we are 'Foreign Workers.'"

"And it means?"

"That we are foreign workers."

"Foreign workers, they must be joking. We are prisoners, that's what we are! We did not ask to be here, or for a job."

"Oh Gala! Stop! Ha...ha...I am sorry, but you sounded so funny, I know, I know! We should not draw attention!"

"What's so funny, young lady? Or is something wrong?" asked the old soldier escorting us to the tracks.

"No, Sir, everything is fine, just fine," Maria answered politely. "Pshss... I told you to be careful. Gala, come close, I don't want to speak loudly, and we don't want anyone listening. Careful now, we are at the truck. There are two armed soldiers. We do not want to annoy them; we will speak later."

"Yes, you are right Maria, we must be more careful. Germans can be so unpredictable."

Maria looked at me, puzzled, with her eyes wide open. "What do you mean, Gala?"

"Later, I will tell you later, come let's get up. You are right. We do not won't to annoy them."

We climbed into the truck, where eight other women were sitting. I could not see Nina and had this feeling that I might not see her again for a long time, if ever.

"Where is Nina? She is not here."

"I saw her climbing on to the other truck. I am sure I saw her. Do not worry. She will be fine; she is in one of the trucks. Come on, we had better hurry and find a seat. This is an evil place, the quicker we are out of here the better."

I was worried, feeling scared and lost, and even the presence of my new friend could not give me enough comfort. No matter how much Nina and I fought we loved each other, and she was all I had left of my family. I tried to sound brave when I spoke to Maria.

"Since we left home Nina is not the same. It is as if she lost her soul, her spirit is gone. She always tried to push me around, but not now. I am worried about her."

Maria put her arm around my shoulders and whispered gently in my ear "This war is affecting us all; it is affecting us in different ways but is affecting everyone. I was enrolled in first year to study architecture, and now this. I do not know where my family is or what has happened to them."

I looked at Maria's face and saw for the first time that she was not smiling. Tears were rolling down her cheeks and I realised that my fears stopped me from noticing that my friend was also scared and lost. I tried to comfort her and squeezed her hand before saying "We should call ourselves lucky that we are alive. Look what happened to my friend Pola and her family and many others. Finally, we are moving."

The truck increased speed and soon we were travelling on a country road.

"Thank God! I could not stand this stench. What a horrible place this Dachau is." Maria squeezed my hand back and we both found comfort in each other. We saw that other trucks were following us, but if Nina was in one of them, I didn't know. Ten minutes later the truck entered a forest. At the beginning it was clear, and we could see sunshine through the branches of the trees. Soon this changed and we travelled on a narrow dirt road in the middle of a dense forest with tall thick trees. The sun disappeared; the air was humid and smelling of fungus.

Maria looked me seriously and asked me "Gala, where do you think they are taking us?"

"I do not know Maria! I do not know."

We went silent, lost in our thoughts as I was wondering where we were going and what was waiting in front of us? Would I see Nina, father, or my brothers again? Would I ever return home? Then I put my head on Maria's comforting shoulders and fell into a deep and dreamless sleep. Suddenly I woke up; Maria was shaking me by my shoulders.

I was afraid when I investigated the darkness and noticed that four women were missing, and the truck was standing still. Maria covered my mouth with her hand and pushed me to the back of the truck. We sat behind the other women in silence. Our guards were not there. Maria was shaking and holding me tight.

She spoke quietly. "Gala, when the soldiers come back pretend that you are asleep.

"What's the matter Maria? Why are you so scared?"

"I do not know what exactly is happening? I was asleep and I was woken up by one of the soldiers. He was pulling on my arm, and when one of the women told him to go outside with her, they both left laughing. I think that the other soldiers are with the other three women."

I raised the collar of my overcoat to make myself invisible and stop breathing when the women and soldiers came back. The four were panting and flushed. They took their seats quickly and the truck started moving and jumping again. I was sitting in an uncomfortable position, my whole body was aching, and I was very hungry and cold. I tried to cover my naked feet with my coat that was too short, but Maria and I were happy that the truck didn't stop again. It was dark outside and every so often we could glimpse the dim lights of a house passing by. I stirred and whispered to my friend.

"Where are we, Maria?"

"I do not know, Gala. But we must be approaching a factory; can you hear the noise of machinery?"

Now that Maria mentioned it I started hearing the noise of a factory. Soon we left this behind us and again it was pitch dark. The only noise we could hear was that of the engine of the truck. A short time later the truck stopped and we heard a male voice shouting something and laughter, then 'Heil Hitler!'

We started moving again for a very short time. The two soldiers who were guarding us jumped out and with a hand motion signalled us to leave the track. It was a good feeling, standing again on the ground and to be able to stretch our stiff bodies. At the same time, we were terrified about what might happen to us.

Four

We were standing in front of a set of houses, Maria, I and eight other women. Some of the houses were two storey stone or brick; others were buildings of wood. All the houses were surrounded by a wire fence. The soldiers escorted us inside a wooden house next to the wire fence and as soon we were inside, they left. We stood in a large dormitory with single iron beds lining both sides of the room, twelve in total. Two women were in the room, and as soon as the door closed behind the soldiers, the silence broke. They both started talking at the same time.

"Where do you come from? What is happening at the front? What are your names? And the magic question, "Are you hungry?"

There was soup and bread. The soup was a mess of potatoes and carrots cooked together and thickened with flour, the bread coarse rye. As we warmed up and were eating the soup, life started to come back into our stiff bodies. We hadn't eaten a cooked meal for weeks and Maria warned me.

"Slow down Gala, or you will get sick. Do not overeat."

I slowed down, embarrassed by my greedy behaviour, but when I was offered seconds I didn't refuse. The two women turned out to be French; Nicole and Juliet, and they did not speak Russian but a bit of German. Until today I still don't know how we communicated. But we managed with Maria and a Polish woman called Stasia; they both spoke French and translated. We chatted for a while and before going to bed Nicole passed me a bucket with warm water and washing soap. And she directed me to where I could wash.

At the back was a door that to a small room no more than two square meters and inside was another bucket that was used as a toilet. Someone had cut a small hole in the floor where the water could drain. I washed my body vigorously, soaping and rubbing until I was red. I wasn't washing only the dirt but all the experiences and memories from the last weeks. Probably I would have rubbed my skin off if Maria had not called me to hurry up. She and the others wanted to wash too. Later in the darkness of the room, lying on a bed for first time since I left home and feeling extremely lost and lonely, I started to cry. I felt lost and could not understanding why humans stopped being human. Why did those things happen to me? I wanted to be home with my family or at least with my brothers fighting the Germans, but instead I was in this inhospitable place. I must have cried myself into a dark and dreamless sleep. When I woke up, I was looking into Maria's smiling face.

"Get up, your sleepy head, we must hurry. Here, put this on. We are going to work." She was dressed in grey overalls that were much too big and was wearing heavy boots. The other women were dressed in similar clothing. After I washed in a basin and dressed in overalls like the others someone passed me a slice of bread and a cup of weak and bitter tea.

I never could get used to drinking bitter tea. As soon as we finished our frugal breakfast, we went outside where another forty women were forming in a semicircle. Two uniformed men were standing in front of us. One was very young and correctly dressed; the older soldier that later I found out was the Commandant was standing provocatively with spread legs. He was wearing trousers and an open shirt, with no jacket, and holding an open bottle of brandy in his right hand. He looked like someone that just had woken up, but also looking drunk. He had two small, fish-like eyes in a red and swollen face. His lips were a thin line and overall, he looked revolting.

The younger soldier started counting us, as if we were animals and did not have names. I never could get used to it. I resigned myself to my fate, but not completely. Inside me, I felt anger and indignation that I started to express with my body language. I always stood very straight and looked very proud, because I knew something they, the soldiers, did not know. I knew that my brothers were chasing them out of my country. This knowledge, and the promise I gave to Nina, gave me the strength to survive.

Although, on this first day in Gross-Ottersleben, the situation in my country still looked grim. Deep in my mind, I was hoping that the war would change and that the losers would, in the end, be the winners. I was then very young. Only later did I learn that in a war there are never winners, only losers.

After they counted us we were escorted to the trucks that were waiting outside on the street, but before we reached the gate something happened. A group of five women in front of us slowed down as they were walking next to the Commandant. Apparently one of them made some nasty comment about him, and the others laughed at it. He must have heard it because one second later, he was holding her by the hair and was kicking her.

We were urged to hurry and climb into the truck. From there we heard her screams, but the truck started moving very fast, and I had difficulty keeping my balance. Someone helped me to sit on the bench. The truck that I, Maria, Nicole, and Juliet climbed into was half occupied by other prisoners, who to our surprise were some ten young men. They were prisoners of war, and from different parts of Europe. As soon as we were seated someone shouted something in French and they all started laughing. I went tense. My knowledge of French was very limited, and I only understood that he had shouted something in reference to Maria and me.

Nicole and Juliet were also laughing, and Maria joined in, so I relaxed and soon I was lost in a conversation with a compatriot of mine. His name was Boris and he was a joiner from Kharkov who had been visiting his older sister in Kiev. Three weeks ago Germans arrested him in the market when he was queuing for some vegetables. He was a nice person and a good observer, because he noticed my apprehension.

"What's wrong Gala? Why are you so quiet? I know it may sound very silly and you must have more than one thing to worry about. But there is not much you can do for now and things are not too bad here. They need workers in the factory, and they treat us reasonably well there. Cheer up Galinka!" he added before jumping down from the truck. We had arrived at the factory. I wanted to respond but only managed a quick smile. No one talked about the woman left behind at the mercy of the Commandant. As if it never happened.

"Came on Gala, stop daydreaming! We must hurry up!" Maria was pulling on my sleeve. We jumped off the truck and as we passed the main entry to the factory, I noticed that six armed soldiers guarded it. Later I found out that more soldiers guarded the factory, posted in different strategic places. The factory was a big complex of long one-story buildings lined up behind the administration block, a two-story brick building in which the director's office was located. We were escorted inside one of the barracks. Inside the building was lined with different machinery and workbenches.

The night shift workers were still working. They left soon and the day shift workers took over. Everyone seemed to know what to do. Maria, I and the other four women were standing lost in this big hall. A tall blond man in his late thirties approached us. Surprisingly he was not dressed in a uniform.

He told us to follow him and took us to the bench that, from now on, Maria and I would work on. He showed us how to assemble shells and bullets and told us that if we had any problems not to hesitate to ask him. It was strange to hear a German person be polite, and instead of shouting something incoherent and intimidating, be reasonable.

Yes, it put all my experience of the Germans into another perspective. Instead of just Germans, there were these Germans and those Germans, and it made me feel human again. We had to assemble the ammunition, fill it with explosive, and check the balance and weight. Then we would send it to the next bench where it was packed. We worked the whole day with a short lunch break, long enough to eat a piece of bread and soup served in an old metal bowls. The soup was of no distinctive taste. It consisted of some mushy mixture of onions and potatoes. Sometimes a bit of fat was swimming on top.

At the beginning the soup was reasonable, but as the war went on, the quality of the soup diminished. The first thing I did after the war was to stop eating soup. Once a week at the camp we all were given a ration of potatoes, onions and bread, some flour and fat, and sometimes we had carrots or parsnips. It never was enough, and we were always hungry. After the evening meal, we would wash our underwear and wash ourselves the best we could in the small basin. We had clothes-lines hanging from wall to wall and inside the house.

Sometimes we would splash water on each other, instead of a bath. As always ended with lots of laughter, and usually the older women would join in. That first evening, after returning from the factory to the camp we cooked soup for our evening meal. By the time we finished with our chores it was late and Juliet started to hurry as up.

"Come on Gala, Maria! Hurry up! We must be in bed before pig-face gets here. If he finds us out of bed, he will beat us up. *Dies Schwein!*"

I did not understand what she meant and asked her what she meant. Who would come and why was she so scared?

She responded abruptly "Go to bed. I will explain tomorrow."

I looked around the room. All the women were in bed, including my friend Maria, and for once I decided that the best thing could do was what I was told. Just as soon as I covered myself with a blanket, the door opened wide, and the Commandant stood there with other three soldiers. The room was deathly silent. I could hear my own heartbeats. The Commandant stood there for few minutes, and he laughed out loud, a horrible-sounding laugh that gave me goose bumps, and before leaving he turned the light off. I lay in bed paralysed with fear, feeling hot and sweating. It was a cold winter night. Next day Juliet spoke to me before leaving for work.

"I am glad that you were in bed when the pig arrived". I started convulsively laughing when she said 'Pig'. Finally, I understood what she meant. I was bending now laughing and the other women joined in. For a while the room vibrated with the sound of laughter that was like escape from a long tension. After breakfast we hurried off, all eager to go to work and meet the male prisoners.

They were living on the other side of the camp with a wire fence dividing us. I felt safer when the male prisoners were around, although they were in the same vulnerable position that we were. Perhaps I was relating them to my brothers and father who were always protective of me. Boris was in the truck, and it became a ritual that as soon I climbed on to the truck Boris would sit next to me and we would chat about any subject. Sometimes it was only he who was talking, telling me about the wonderful things his three-months old baby son could do and how much he was missing him and his young wife.

Hearing Boris with his moods swinging would not last for long. And soon he would be joking and cheering us all up again. As time passed Maria and I learned more about the place where we were now living. Our house was the last house of the complex of six houses next to the wire fence that divided us from the men's camp. Living in the last house turned out to be quite convenient. First, the Commandant would sometimes miss out checking on us. Later we found out that it was also an easy escape route to meet with the male prisoners. There was no point in trying to escape from the camp. We were in the middle of Germany and easily caught and the punishment would be, if not to be shot, sent to places that were worse than where we were living. Resigned to our destinies we tried to live the best we could, avoiding the Commandant as much as possible. He was very violent towards women and more so when he was drunk, which he was nearly every day. Also, we learned that some of the women prisoners were better avoided.

There was a small group of seven women who joined the Commandant and his cronies in drinking orgies. I do not know if they were forced to it or did so because they would get some privileges. Whatever the reason they were very nasty to the other prisoners, and we were told to avoid getting involved with them.

In the house that we shared the women were nice, and small groups formed. Juliet, Maria, Nicole and I were the youngest. The other eight women, whose ages were between thirty and forty, started mothering us after a few days, but we did not mind. Three women were from Poland, and the other five were from Ukraine. Nicole was the oldest of the four of us, she was twenty-four. Blond and very quiet, she also was discreet. She was not in any way unfriendly. We could always count on her, and she was always willing to help. I liked her, although we hardly ever spoke to each other.

One day Juliet arrived from the factory very excited and with red cheeks. She was humming the tune of a French love song. *Le nuit, toujours, toujours, je t'aime* and then she shouted "I am in love! I am in love!"

She started laughing and dancing around the room until she ran out of breath and collapsed on a chair. We surrounded her and started questioning. "Who is he? Do we know him? Is he good looking?"

But Juliet only laughed and then she said "Tomorrow, I will tell you everything, not today. I am meeting him tonight."

We all started talking at the same time. "No, you cannot do that. It is too dangerous, the night guards can kill you if they see you and, if not, think what the Commandant will do to you when he finds out."

No matter what we said, Juliet would not listen. She had made her mind up and she was going! No argument could persuade her. She went to bed with her clothes on, covered up to her chin with the blanket when the Commandant arrived to check on us and turn the lights off. Luckily, he didn't notice anything unusual and as soon as he left Juliet ran to the back window of the toilet, opened it, and climbed out. We saw her in the morning and to me, she didn't look any different, except that she was laughing more. She looked happy.

She told us that her lover was from Poland, and his name was Jan. I knew him, he worked at a lathe, but we had never spoken to each other. Jan was tall, blond and very good-looking, and with many female admirers. This by itself could create problems I thought. Possibly there would be lots of broken female hearts. But I didn't talk to anyone about it, and in the house we were all happy for Juliet. One evening, around Christmas, Juliet pulled her violin from under her bed and started to play a Christmas song.

I joined in and started to sing it. After we finished the women started to applaud and Juliet told me that I sang very well.

She didn't finish, as the door was opened violently and the Commandant stood there. His face was red, and he looked fiercely at us in silence, which was scarier than if he had yelled. We didn't know what he was going to do to us, but for once he decided to do nothing. He turned towards the door, and shouted "Sleep now, go to sleep", and turned the lights off.

Next day one of the soldiers told us that when the Commandant heard us singing he stopped in surprise behind the door, listening until we stopped playing and singing. After the Commandant left the room, Juliet asked me if I would sing in the factory.

"When would you like me to sing?" I asked.

"Tomorrow, Gala. It is Christmas, didn't you know?"

No, I did not know. These things had ceased to be important here. This was the second Christmas that we were spending far away from home and it felt like eternity. God, I wished the war was over. When I said this to Juliet she replied "Me too, my dear, but it is not over, and we may as well have some fun if we can."

"Alright, dear Juliet, I will sing tomorrow as I never did before. I promise, but tell me, what shall I sing?"

"Do you know the song 'Quiet night, holy night'?"

"Yes, I do."

"Good! We will start with that and then we will see, but now we shall sleep. Good night, Gala."

"Good night, Juliet, I must say that I am starting to be excited about tomorrow."

The next day when the night shift arrived to take over from our shift, Juliet pulled out her violin and started playing. After she played a few notes everything and everybody went silent and then I joined in. The machines stopped and only the sound of the violin and my voice could be heard. I believe that this was my best performance. Many people told me that night that I sang beautifully. After we finished, they all applauded and asked us to play and sing more, which we did.

I was singing a third song when food appeared on one of the benches. It was a very simple food, just bread, apples, and some stew with some meat, but to us this was a big feast. It did not last for too long, and we had to eat in haste. The escort soldiers started urging us to hurry up. We had to be in the camp, and we were two hours late. They did not want the Commandant to get impatient and call the SS men to investigate our disappearance. When we arrived at the camp they told the Commandant that the truck broke down.

Some Germans were in fear of the SS men, just as we prisoners were of them. As the war progressed and the Germans were losing battles we were pushed at the factory to increase production. We had to work harder, but we were still treated well by the supervisor. We heard that in the other buildings of the factory some supervisors were not as nice as ours and we called ourselves lucky. At the beginning there were some other German workers in the factory, and they would talk to us and share some food with us. But gradually they disappeared from the factory, probably required as soldiers and sent to the front. Who knows? Maybe the collaborators of the Gestapo or SS told on them, and they were deliberately removed. It was against their politics to be nice to the prisoners. Regardless of this, our supervisor would often stop next to me where I was working and ask questions about how I was going at work. But sometimes he would ask personal questions about my family or about my country.

He also always had a piece of fruit or a piece of bread in his pocket, which he never gave directly to me. He would leave them on our bench as if by accident. Once he left some sweets; it was such a luxury. Maria was always there to translate when I was stuck with my German, which was progressing slowly.

Five

Juliet was a beautiful woman with black shoulder length hair and shining green eyes; her skin was porcelain white which looked nearly transparent. She moved with such elegance and flexibility that she reminded me of a black wild cat. She had good teeth and smiled a lot. One night she told me her story of how she ended in Gross-Ottersleben.

She had just moved in June 1940 from Tours to Paris, two weeks before the Germans marched in. She was sharing a flat with Henri, who was a school friend, and was studying at the Sorbonne University. The flat was spacious, quiet and convenient. It was situated in the Rue Froidevaux, opposite the Montparnasse Cemetery and not far from the university. Henri told Juliet that it belonged to an aunt who was visiting her daughter in America.

"My dear Juliet, as things are looking now, I do not think she will return from America very soon, so we can call ourselves lucky. Rent-free accommodation in Paris these days is a commodity not many have."

"I know, I know! I will make sure that it will be always clean and tidy, so when she returns from America the flat will look nice."

She started working in a cafeteria as a waitress during the daytime. In the evenings Henri and she would cook together. Usually after dinner, Henri would go out and return late into the night. He would not tell her where he was going, and she did not ask. When Henri was not there, she would read or play the violin. She had played since the age of five. One day around April 1941, she returned from work and found three German cars stationed in front of the entry to her apartment block. Soldiers stood on guard and others were unloading big suitcases from one of the cars. The guards stopped her when she was about to enter the building, asked her for documentation and started questioning her.

What was she doing there? She was about to explain that she was living upstairs when a Colonel got out of one of the cars and gave an order to the soldiers. They stopped interrogating her and gestured to her to enter. As she ran up the stairs to her apartment on the second floor she noticed that the doors of the apartment below hers were wide open. The German Colonel was moving into this apartment. Only when she closed the doors of her apartment did she notice how scared she was and that she was shivering. Her reflection in the mirror on the wall of entrance looked pale and sick. She went into lounge room and lit the fire. Then she took her violin out of the case and slowly started to play. It was a piece by Paganini, one she knew well. Finally, she felt calm and warm.

Kurt Habel was a colonel in the Wehrmacht responsible for supplies and administration. His status permitted him to rent an apartment and he preferred to have his own place instead of spending his free time with other officers. Now, as he was giving orders to his soldiers about where to put his luggage, he heard the violin. He stopped in the middle of the room and, as the noise of the soldiers was interfering with the sound of the music, he dismissed them. In the silence of his apartment, he could hear the clarity and the fidelity of the performance. He knew about music; before he joined the army he had studied music in Heidelberg, but that was a long time ago.

He had been driving his new car to a picnic with his beautiful girlfriend Lizzy. It was his parents' present for Christmas 1928. He saw the other car just as he came out of the bend. It was on the wrong side of the road and within seconds the architecture of his life shifted forever. He was the only survivor.

After months in hospital he left Heidelberg and moved to Berlin. He joined the Wehrmacht and became a soldier at a time when serving in the army was an honour. Now he was not so sure. He waved his hand in the air as if wanting to send his thoughts away. The sound of this beautiful performance had filled him with emotion and brought memories of pain. He began to hate being a soldier and he hated this useless war, but he was a man of honour. His breathing slowed and his heartbeat accelerated, and he threw his body into the armchair and lost himself completely in the music. It became a routine that, first thing after work, on his arrival home, Juliet would play a piece of music. After she finished playing, she would change her working clothes to something more comfortable and would wait for Henri or start to prepare a meal.

What Julie did not know was that in the apartment below Kurt Habel would religiously arrive home ten minutes early, serve himself a drink and then wait on the sofa for the music to start. Julie arrived home earlier than usual one afternoon. She had a cold, was shivering, had a high temperature and a red running nose and was in no state to play the violin. She ran a hot bath and went straight to bed with a cup of bitter tasting herbal tea. That night Kurt waited for a long time for the sounds of the violin. He sat there and waited. He left the dinner which Werner, his attendant, served him untouched and he must have drunk himself into a stupor. The dim light of sunrise found him in the armchair fully dressed and a glass of brandy still in his hand.

When, next evening, the violin stayed silent he felt despair and disappointment. Two days later he could not wait any longer and went upstairs to knock on the door of Juliet and Henri's apartment.

Henri opened the door and was surprised to see Kurt. The two men stared at each other for a moment before Henri finally managed to say, in a low voice "Please, what can I do for you?"

A hundred thoughts went through his mind. Was he in danger? Was this German looking for him? He did not look on duty. The buttons of his jacket were open and now Kurt smiled with a look of embarrassment on his face.

"I was wondering what had happened to the violinist that I was listening to every afternoon. Why did you stop playing?"

Surprisingly, he said it in fluent French. Henri was standing there smiling, realising that he had been mistaken for the violin player. He responded nervously but also with relief. "You mean Juliet; she is the musician, not me. She is sick in bed, with a cold. Perhaps tomorrow she will play again."

"Yes, I will wait! Tell the lady please, that she is an excellent violinist. I wish her a quick recovery, and please forgive my intrusion." Kurt turned and started slowly to descend to the floor below. Juliet's cold lasted another five days. On Friday afternoon, before she had left her bed and was not completely recovered, the doorbell rang. She did not expect such an extravagant sight: baskets of roses of all imaginable colours and in, front of her, a smiling German colonel.

Juliet felt self-conscious. She was wearing a pair of old pyjamas covered by an ancient and discoloured dressing gown. Her normally long straight hair looked like a bird's nest. Her nose was still red and her face blotched. She felt embarrassed as he was asking if he and his attendant Werner could come in. Juliet only then noticed that an older soldier was standing behind the baskets of flowers. She stepped aside making a sign with for them to come in and spoke. "Please come in but be warned this place is in a state of mess, just like me." She sneezed again into a hanky.

They went in, the attendant placed the baskets around the sitting room and Kurt dismissed him. Werner left silently and closed the door behind him. Juliet and Kurt were staring at each other. The room was silent until Juliet broke in with a question. "Would you like a cup of tea?"

"Yes, please," responded Kurt.

Juliet left the room and Kurt started looking with interest at his surroundings. The lounge room was spacious. A piano stood in one corner, next to a large glass folding door. Small baroque chairs, five in all, surrounded a small table of the same style in another corner. A large sofa and two armchairs were standing in the middle of the room. Juliet's violin was lying in an open case that was lying on one of the armchairs. Two large lead-glass cabinets stood on each side of the door leading into corridor through which Juliet had left. Kurt approached the piano and noticed through the small opening in the glass door a large library. He opened the piano and, instinctively, without being able to explain why, he started to play Brahms' Sonata No 2 in A major.

At the beginning his fingers felt stiff and, for the first passage, he was shaking with an unexplained emotion. Slowly he started to relax, and his playing became firmer and more confident. Juliet arrived with the tea and silently placed it on the small table. Smiling she pulled out her violin and joined in. The sound of music filled the room with energy. Both the man and the woman seemed transfixed. They were talking to each other through the music. They had a language that was above the ordinary and beyond words; they played every note with passion and love for the music.

The dim light of the room was sometimes interrupted by the purple shimmers of the sunset. The boundaries of status and nationality melted away, the war and time stood still, there was only their music. When the last noted of music fell into silence they did not move. Kurt stayed seated; tears were running down his face. He was shaken into his deepest self. Juliet stood there very confused, looking at Kurt. She did not see the enemy but a gentle person who loved music, just like her. She smiled and asked, "Shall I make us a fresh cup of tea? This one went cold, I am afraid."

There was movement in the room, and they heard a gentle cough, which made them both turn in surprise. Henri, who had arrived a while before, silently sat in one of the armchairs. He too had felt trapped by the magic of the afternoon. Now he stood up and bowed to them, saying "I am in debt to both of you. I will make fresh tea."

Soon all three, two young people and a middle-aged man, were drinking tea and having a pleasant conversation about music and other subjects. As if by an unspoken agreement they did not mention the war. After this evening it became a routine that every afternoon Kurt would go upstairs. Juliet and he would play their chosen music. Sometimes Henri would arrive home early and join them with a cup of tea. Some evenings they would join Kurt for dinner that Werner prepared. On those occasions Henri and Kurt would play a game of chess afterwards. At the back of their minds, they must have known that this idyllic existence could not last forever. Perhaps for this reason they very much enjoyed every moment of each other's company.

In July 1941, two days before Juliet's birthday, Kurt arrived at their apartment holding a big packet and two tickets to the Theatre de l'Opera. "They are performing Madame Butterfly on Friday," he said, "and you are both invited. This is my birthday present to Juliet. We will dine afterwards at Suboise."

He passed the packet to the speechless Henri and left. Juliet eager opened it and found an evening suit with matching white shirt for Henri and an elegant long green dress. Juliet went to spend two weeks of her wages on a pair of matching shoes. On Friday evening Werner came up and told them that a car had arrived to take them to the theatre. The driver told them that Kurt had been delayed and would meet them in the foyer. At the theatre, the two soldiers who were guarding the entry saluted and after seeing their tickets, let them in.

Before they entered the theatre Henri noticed that heavily armed soldiers were surrounding the theatre and the vicinity. The foyer was packed with elegantly dressed men and women. There were many high-ranking Germans officers with their female companions. Diplomats represented their countries, some wearing their traditional costumes made of rich silks and brocades. There was a lot of glitter and colours.

Kurt was standing on the steps of the main stairs, looking very well in full uniform. He was talking with a diplomat when he spotted Juliet and Henri. He approached them quickly, a wide smile on his face, took Juliet's hand to his lips and spoke. "Mademoiselle, you look stunning. Tonight, everyone's eyes in this place are on you."

Saying this he offered her his arm. He smiled at Henri and saluted him with a nod of his head. They went to take their seats. During the interval Kurt introduced them to many people. Juliet could not remember any of the names. After the performance they went straight to Suboise, where they had a magnificent dinner and champagne. Juliet danced alternately with Kurt and Henri, and it was long past midnight when they got home.

This extraordinary evening would stay in Juliet's memory for ever. But unfortunately it also stayed in the memory of the Gestapo, who started to be interested in who they were and how they were related to Kurt. They asked Vichy to investigate and few weeks later the Vichy Police arrived asking for Henri. They left a card with a phone number and a message for Henri to contact them. The same day Henri disappeared and when he failed to return for three days, Juliet told Kurt and he promised to find out what had happened. Next day there was a raid on their apartments and the Vichy Police confiscated everything they could put they fingers on. Luckily Juliet's violin was downstairs in Kurt's apartment and Juliet was at work.

That evening, when she arrived home and found the mess, she just sat on the floor and cried. Kurt arrived and took her to his apartment and there he told her that someone from the Gestapo in conjunction with the Vichy police had investigated who they were. They had discovered Henri's involvement with the Resistance. They had arrested him, and the Gestapo was interrogating him. An order was out for her arrest.

Kurt had managed to take over her case and to save her from the Gestapo's hands and was sending her next morning to one of Germany's Labour Camps. He also told her that he believed in her innocence and didn't judge Henri either.

"In his place I would do the same, try to liberate my country."

That night she slept in Kurt's bed and for this one night they were lovers.

Six

One morning I noted a new face in the truck on our way to the factory. Boris introduced me to this new prisoner, whose name was George, and to whom I immediately felt very attracted. He had a warm deep voice which had a calming effect on me. His big blue eyes would look at my face intensely. Oh, I get shivers just remembering his beautiful eyes. I found out that he was from Lyon in France and that he spoke reasonable German, some English and some Russian. Later I found that he also was fluent in Czech, as this was where he was born. His parents had moved to France shortly before the First World War, when he was a small toddler.

Soon it became clear to me that I was deeply in love with him. If I could have spent every minute with him I would. Which was not so easy, as a wire fence separated us in the camp and in the factory we had to work. Only during the short lunch breaks at the factory could we exchange some words with each other and then I also wasn't sure if he responded to my feelings. Just in case, I kept a safe distance between us. I do not know how I managed to hide my feelings for such a long time and survive all those internal torments.

One evening, on our way back to the camp he left his seat, asked Boris to swap with him and sat next to me. I could hardly breathe and felt quite dizzy.

"How are you, Gala? A beautiful name for a beautiful woman."

My face must have been red. I could feel the heat and only managed a short *thank you.*

"I heard that you sing very well," he continued complimenting me.

"Yes, I do a bit. Before the war I was admitted to the School of Music in Kiev, but before I even started the war broke out and here I am."

He looked at me for a while in silence and then he asked "Could you? Would you please sing for us now?"

I loved singing and still do, so I didn't need to be persuaded. First I sang an aria from Verdi and then a Ukrainian song. Everyone went silent for a while, as if my singing had taken them another place and another time and inside their own internal world. When I finished singing everyone applauded, even the German soldiers that were guarding us.

George took my hand and squeezed it gently. We sat so for a while, and I could feel the warmth of his hand. It was such a wonderful feeling as if we were somewhere else, just George and me. I didn't move, afraid that if I did this moment would stop. I wished we could stay like this forever. I wished that the truck would never get to its destination and that moment could last for ever (something that I partly managed as this moment stayed with me for ever). Before the truck stopped, he put his head close to mine and whispered in my ear.

"I would like to meet with you alone. What do you think? Could we meet?"

"I don't know, I...it is dangerous and as much I would like to, I do not know how," I responded.

"You do like me! Oh Galinka! I was worried you might reject me."

The biggest smile I ever saw spread over his face. His whole face was smiling, and he looked into my eyes like no one ever did. His eyes were of an intense blue and I saw a look of admiration and love, but also of desire. I could see myself in his eyes as if in the clear water of a river. I could see my reflection and I saw that I was beautiful. We could not part our eyes from each other, and I wanted to drown in the depth of his lips. I started to shiver, feeling cold and my skin had goose bumps again. Then he took my hand into again his and his hand was transmitting security. I started to calm down but when he asked me again if I would come to meet him that night by the wire fence, I only managed a nod.

As soon as we got into our room Maria, Nicole and Juliet started pestering me. They were bombarding me with hundreds of questions.

"Since when are you in love with George? Why didn't you tell us?"

This went on for a whole evening, until we went to bed. After the *Commandant* did his rounds, Juliet and I slipped out through the back window and ran to the wire fence. A large tree covered one part of the fence and Jan was waiting on the other site. He lifted the wire fence and we slipped through.

After we got to the other side, he led us to one of the barracks. Soon we were in a dark room. George was there. He took my hands into his, and mine were shaking again.

I was very scared, but at the same time I was longing for George. He must have noticed how scared I was, because when we sat down on the floor, he just put his arm around my shoulders, and we sat there. For a long time, we sat there in silence, he gently stroking my arm, and finally he broke the silence by asking about my family and my country and how I ended up in this place.

I told him about my friend Pola and what happened to her family and the others. His arm tightened round my shoulders, as if wanting to protect me. It felt so good, and I felt safe. Finally, he said "How could they do this to women and children? What kind of people are they? They behave very civilised among themselves, so why are they like this to others?"

"You know, I thought at first that all Germans were like this, but now I have learnt that not all Germans are bad people. I know that some Ukrainians were involved in the killing."

"I know, I know, the Vichy Police is as bad as the Germans."

George held me more tightly. He put his cheek against mine, which was fire hot. His was cool and smooth. He must have shaved just before meeting with me. George was saying that he loved me and that I was beautiful. Then he took my face in his hands and our lips found each other for a first kiss that lasted for a long time.

I was in a dream from which I didn't want to wake up; his tongue was savouring my mouth and I was shivering. His hands were caressing my body, our kisses intensified, and he started to unbutton my blouse. Slowly I started responding to his caresses, shyly at first, but then with a passion that surprised me. He was slowly kissing my whole body. I was floating and wishing time to stand still, and at that moment I felt a strong pain followed by immense pleasure. His body was pressing against me and before I lost consciousness, I felt him tremble and heard him call out my name.

"Gala, darling, how are you?" he was whispering into my ear, biting it gently and I didn't want to wake up so soon. I told him that and that I loved him, and I did. We stayed in each other's arms kissing and George told me how he became a member of the resistance in Lyon.

This only happened after the Vichy Police killed his younger brother. His brother was very young, still in college. He went to attend an assembly that was organised by the Communist party. The irony was he didn't belong to the party; he was just escorting a female friend. After his death George joined the Resistance. Two months before they had tried to blow up a goods train from Germany that was transporting ammunition supplies. They must have been betrayed because the Vichy Police was waiting there and arrested them. Two of his companions were killed when they started to escape. He and two others were sent to Germany. In the darkness, I heard Juliet calling me urgently, saying that we had to go now. It was so difficult to part from George, not knowing if we were going to see each other again.

"Gala, I will see you tomorrow, yes, we will. I miss you already."

Juliet and I returned to our room without any problem and from then on, every second or third night, Juliet and I would slip into the men's camp. This worked well, and for one month I was floating in the air from happiness; George was such a magnificent lover. He was gentle and he was deeply in love with me. And for the first time since the Gestapo picked me up at my home I felt content, if only for a very short time. I did not think about the future, I didn't know if it existed and didn't care. My only concern was the present.

Then one night when Juliet and I had just returned to our room, we heard the Commandant and his cronies approaching our house. It was twelve o'clock. It was unusual that he would come round so late. We had no time to undress, and we jumped into bed dressed and with our shoes still on.

We were covered up to our chins with the blankets. I could hear my heart pumping like crazy. The Commandant checked that we all were in bed. He walked at slow pace in the middle of the room. Everything was fine and he was about to leave when the unthinkable happened. One of my shoes got loose and it fell with a damp noise to the floor. In one second the Commandant was over me; he pulled the blanket off and then he pulled me by my head and hair to the floor. His face was red, his eyes had a glassy look and his breath stank of alcohol.

He was full of rage, screaming names at me.

"I will kill you! You whore, you want sex I will give you sex. Here, take this, you beast."

He started kicking me with his heavy boots all over my body. The pain was so severe that I vomited and was bleeding from my mouth. The women started screaming that he was going to kill me, and probably he would have, if I hadn't fainted.

When I woke up, I was looking straight into Maria's serious face. Next to her were Juliet and Nicole. They started talking all at the same time.

"How are you? Are you in pain?" Nicole was asking if I could speak.

"Oh! Galinka, Galinka!" Maria started crying, "I didn't take good care of you, what will Nina say?"

I wanted to respond that it was not her fault but could not; my mouth was swollen, and I was missing one molar on my left side. I was grateful when one of the older women, Stasia, silenced my friends and started looking after me. Apparently, she was a nurse in Poland and knew what she was doing. She touched every part of my body, to find any fractured bones or internal injuries.

Once this was done, she said "You will be fine, but you will have lots of pain for a few days."

She then applied cold wet cloths to my face and other parts of my body. This gave me some relief, and she asked Maria to change them every hour. Next morning and for the following weeks, travelling to the factory was a torture; each time the truck jumped I felt a strong pain in the kidney region. I also felt very embarrassed, my face was swollen, and I looked awful. George was very kind and did his best to comfort me, and so were the others. Boris brought a blanket under his shirt; he put it on the bench in the truck so I could find some comfort.

Soon I started to feel better, but I was scared to venture another trip into the men's camp. The Commandant would check our house every day, sometimes twice in the same night and at random hours. It was nerve-breaking: we could be sound asleep when the Commandant would charge in and wake us up. He would throw our blankets off the beds and would swear at us.

"Whores, you are fucking whores, which of you was whoring tonight, which?"

One extremely cold night, two Polish women, Danuta, and Bozena, were sleeping in the same bed. They only wanted to be warm. They didn't have any chance to escape this man. He was over them before they even woke up, kicking them and screaming.

"Now you fuck each other, do you? You want a fuck? You'll get some, yes! You will!"

He called his cronies and they dragged the two poor women out to the Commandant's house. No one slept in the camp; we heard those poor things screaming for a long time. Even in the men's camp they could hear their screams.

Next day on our return from the factory we found Danuta in a fetal position on her bed. God! She looked horrible; her whole face was swollen and bruised and so was every other part of her body. Her vagina and her anus were bleeding; Stasia did whatever she could to save her life but Danuta died next morning. We went behind the house and dug a grave for her when two soldiers, who were our daily escorts on the trucks, arrived. They were carrying Bozena's lifeless and naked body. She was in the same condition as Danuta. We buried them in the same grave. The soldiers stayed with us; one said a prayer. I am sure that they also felt outraged by what had happened. The men on the other side of the fence stood there silent with grim expressions on their faces. Women from other houses joined in. No one cried. We just stood there in silence paying tribute to those two women that died for no crime.

This silence was more powerful than a cry; it was carrying a weight of condemnation. On this day I finally understood why no one cried, fought, or ran away except a small child at Babi Yar, because this powerful silence was denying any form of excuse to the Germans.

This knowledge would haunt those responsible forever. For a whole week the Commandant stayed inside the house. I started to be depressed and was missing George. Without support from Maria, Juliet, and Nicole I do not know how I would have survived. During our trips to the factory and back to the camp, George and I would travel next to each other and hold hands for a short time. His proximity was giving me some comfort. He would tell me each time about how much he was missing me, and sometimes he would ask if I was coming to see him.

I told him that Juliet ventured out on one occasion, and she was nearly caught and was scared to go over. He reassured me that he understood and that he loved me and would wait for however long it took. Oh, it was so difficult.

We started talking about what could be done and someone came up with an idea that we should make an official complaint against the Commandant. Maria and I decided that we would travel to Berlin but we did not speak to anyone about it. We also did not know how and when. In the middle of August we had to work extra hours. They cut our lunchtime to the minimum, and we also noticed a lot of movement in the director's office. One day the Gestapo arrived, and the supervisor was called to the director's office. One hour later he came out practically green in the face. He was very angry, saying.

"They are mad, yes! They are mad!" and then he swore, *Disses Schwein!* Those pigs!

This was very unusual. He never swore. Someone asked him what was wrong? And why was he so angry?

"The Gestapo came here because they think that someone is sabotaging the work. They want us to increase production by double," he responded.

This was bad news. We were working at as fast as we could, our diet was very poor and we were exhausted. We started to use any pretext to move away from our working benches. We would go to the toilet or walk to someone else's bench to find out more news about the war, but it was mainly to have a small break.

I always wondered if this was the reason that Juliet left her workbench. I saw with a glimpse of my eye that she approached Jan's bench with a smile and as I was concentrated on what I was doing, I didn't see what exactly happened. But one moment later, we heard an animal-like scream. The machine that Jan was working on had caught the left sleeve of Juliet's dress. Jan jumped to stop it, but it was too late; seconds later I saw Juliet standing there with a look of disbelief. Her left hand was missing, and her arm was shattered up to her elbow. She was bleeding profusely and where her hand used to be pieces of flesh, skin, white tendons, and blue veins were hanging.

We all stopped what we were doing and rushed to Jan's bench. Someone tied Juliet's arm with a piece of cloth from a shirt. She looked very pale, nearly transparent, and then she looked at us with blurry eyes before passing out. Jan picked her up and he was clutching her gently in his arms. Meanwhile tears were rolling down his cheeks. With a husky voice he was calling her.

"Juliet, *kochana moja,* my darling Juliet, please wake up. Do not leave me! Please!"

Nicole, Maria, and I were holding each other, crying, feeling devastated and without knowing what to do. We felt very inadequate in the face of this tragedy. The ambulance people arrived. The supervisor had called them, and they took Juliet away. We never heard about or saw her again.

She was such a beautiful woman, and I cannot imagine her suffering. The physical pain must have been tremendous but the other pain, worst of all, knowing she would never play the violin again. Jan was devastated. Within hours he aged and became withdrawn and depressed. One week later Maria and I were on our way to Berlin.

Seven

Maria, the three soldiers and I were returning to Gross-Ottersleben, but we were worried. The soldiers took the route to the factory in Magdeburg and went straight to the Director's office. After explaining what happened they saluted and left. The Director looked us in silence through his dark- framed glasses, serious but not unfriendly, and then he said

"You are very brave, but it was not necessary to take so much risk. You should have come earlier to me. I could have investigated the matter."

I felt furious. He knew that something was wrong in the camp; he must have observed that some of us would arrive with bruises and pain that was slowing us down at work. He must have noticed our thin weak bodies and that our performance was low. He never did anything to improve our lives. For such a long time nothing had been done and now he was telling us that he had the power to do something about it.

I remembered what had happened to Juliet. Perhaps her accident could have been prevented. Bozena or Danuta could still have been alive. I felt very angry. I wanted to cry out that he was guilty as much as the Commandant and that he was an accomplice for all the crimes that his compatriots committed by staying silent. I was very angry but decided to hold my tongue. I controlled my anger, and instead I responded.

"Thank you for your thoughtfulness, but we tried not to involve you, or put others at risk."

He smiled and called the supervisor, who took us back with the other prisoners. What an uproar it was! We arrived back escorted by soldiers, and we were fine. We had to answer hundreds of questions: where had we gone? How did we get there and how was it? And it went on and on.

We could have spent days answering all the questions, but we answered only a few. It was time to get back to the camp. Maria and I were very scared, not knowing what would happen. George was silent and he looked angry and when I asked why, he raised his voice.

"What were you thinking? You left without telling me anything! I was here scared to death that something horrible had happened to you and I did not know if I'd ever see you again! Oh Gala! Promise that you will never do such thing again and that in the future you will talk to me. I don't want anything bad to happen to you. I love you!"

He said this with such vehemency that I squeezed his hand in deep emotion and said, before climbing into the truck.

"I promise that I won't ever leave without you again! I promise!"

On our way to the camp in the truck the soldiers that always escorted us to and from the factory told us that the Wehrmacht had picked up the Commandant and he was taken away to the eastern front. Apparently, he protested so much that they grew impatient and did not even let him pack his belongings. We all were cheering and even the soldiers were smiling. No one liked that evil man and everybody was glad that he was not there anymore.

As soon as we arrived we had to assemble in the courtyard under the dim lights. For the first time we were assembling with the men. Five heavily armed soldiers were escorting a middle-aged woman dressed in civilian clothes. She spoke to us and told us that she was the wife of the new Commandant, and her name was *Frau Berg.*

"My husband is down with flu. As soon as he feels better, he will talk to you. For the moment I am here in charge and there will be some changes. The wire that divided both camps has been removed. You can visit each other but I warn you I will not tolerate any fights or any intent of escape. The soldiers have my orders to shoot if you disobey. Otherwise, you may do as you please. You are dismissed."

She left to go inside the house. We were all excited about the news. Never again would we see the hated Commandant. Maria, Nicole, and I clutched each other and cried for Juliet who was with us no more; my whole body was shaken by it. I could not stop, I was crying for Nina, my brothers, and my father when I felt the strong arms of my beloved George. His nearness gave me security and slowly I started to calm down. That night for first time, we stayed the whole night together.

For a couple of weeks there was lots of activity in the camp, as couples started to move in together. There was some need for privacy and the men divided large rooms into smaller dormitories. Kitchens and toilets had to be shared. Some dividers were made only with strings and blankets. Maria was spending those days shaking her head and would say that humans were driven by instinct and not reason.

She could be right. A few months later I discovered that I was pregnant and, I must confess, I had mixed feelings about it. Part of me wanted this baby but another part was wishing it had never happened. I believe I was not the only one feeling that way. We were part of this war, we were undernourished and did not know if we would wake up alive, still less how we would care for a child.

But wonders happen sometimes; another five women were having babies around the same time as me. The knowledge that I wasn't on my own made me feel better, and the fact that the previous Commandant was away and could not terrorise us anymore and that Mrs. Berg oversaw the camp made things better yet.

Before, SS men or the Gestapo would pick up any women that were pregnant and we never saw them again. Then we did not know what had happened to them and we thought that they were sent back home. Only when the war finished, we found out about horrible crimes that our jailers had committed. But now things were a bit better and suddenly I felt that maybe there was some hope and perhaps even a future. George was worried that something bad might happen to me and he became overly protective, to my annoyance.

I started to feel like a doll stuffed with something inside me that must be protected no matter what, no matter what was happening to me, or what would happen. I felt like a guinea pig that everyone was watching closely. And if I showed any kind of emotion, it was always attributed to pregnancy. As if this strange thing that was growing inside my stomach took full power over my personality and I disappeared.

One night Maria woke me up, and she begged me to come and to see Nicole. Nicole had a high temperature, was sweating profusely and was delirious. Sometimes she was calling Juliet's name. At other times she was calling names we had never heard before.

I asked Stasia (who was looking after her) what was wrong.

"I don't know, Gala, but since last week she has complained about headaches."

I remembered then that Nicole had told me few days ago at the factory that she had a headache, but I thought that it had gone away.

"Gala, go and bring me a wet cloth, we must try to get her temperature down."

"Stasia, do you think that you can cure her?" I asked in a wobbly voice while passing the wet cloth to her. She shook her head and added that she needed some medications but also was not quite sure what was wrong with Nicole.

"The only thing we can do for her is put some cold compresses on her forehead and when her temperature drops to cover her with as many blankets we can find."

Maria and I, we stayed with Stasia, and we helped as much as we could to nurse Nicole. Just before dawn Nicole went into crisis, she was shuddering so much that I was afraid she might break some of her bones. Her teeth were chattering, and she was now very cold. Maria got into bed with Nicole, trying to give her heat from her own body.

I started to cry and said to Stasia "There is no hope and sooner or later we're all going to die."

Stasia snapped at me furiously. "There is always hope. Do you hear me, always!"

The other women were looking at us with alarm. Nicole calmed down and shortly after she felt into a deep healing sleep. Only after Stasia reassured us that the worst was over, and Nicole would be fine did we go to bed. Next morning, I was aching all over from lack of sleep, but I was happy that Nicole was getting better. Stasia went to see the Commandant's wife and she agreed that Nicole could stay in bed for the day. Mrs. Berg granted Nicole few days in bed.

This action on Mrs. Berg's part gave me back my hope for the future and the possibility of saving humanity.

Shortly before my time the Commandant's wife asked me to clean her house and do some housework. The job was not too heavy, and I could stop working at the factory. Travelling by truck while pregnant had become difficult and dangerous. The front was closing nearer, and Germany now became the target of severe bombing. It was very scary, and we all were terrified, but at the same time we knew that the war had changed.

The aggressors were now defending themselves and this made some Germans more savage against foreigners. Once, during an air strike, when we were just going to climb into the truck, the siren gave the alarm, and everybody started running to hide in the factory bunker. I went scared and ran to one of the bunkers on the other side of the street. The people in the bunker started to chase me away. One screamed at me "You foreign swine, go away, go away!"

They chased me away; I was seven months pregnant. I started to run in panic and found an entry to a shop. I squashed in there while the bombs were falling and exploding practically next to me.

Next day Mrs. Berg offered me the cleaning job, which I gladly accepted. At the beginning she would leave fruit or biscuits on the table, and once she left some money. I was not interested in money, but the food I hardly managed to resist.

Five days later Mrs. Berg called me to her office and told me "It is all right, you can eat what I left on the table. It is for you to eat, your baby needs some nourishment, and I am happy with the job you are doing here."

As time passed she would leave on the table, apart from food, some underwear, dresses, shoes, and baby clothes. Though these were basic things, they appeared to me luxuries. Some of the clothing I would share with Maria and Nicole.

Under the Commandant's house was a bunker. You could reach it from outside through a heavy wooden door that was under the kitchen window. Inside the house was a corridor that ran between the kitchen and dining room; it had another trap door that also opened to the bunker. The bunker was large and quite deep under the ground. Long stairs led down into it. I assumed that the previous Commandant had built it for himself and his cronies.

I spent lots of time in this bunker and George would stay with me whenever he was in the camp. He was now working double shifts at the factory. On the sixth of June 1944 the Allied Forces landed in Normandy and on the twenty-seventh, I gave birth to my tiny baby daughter in the bunker when we were under heavy bombing. The night of the birth, Mrs. Berg called Stasia. She was only a nurse but here in Gross-Ottersleben, she had become a very good midwife. By the time I gave birth she was an expert.

Nobody prepared me for the pain, and nobody could. When I heard other women screaming when giving birth I thought they were overdoing it. I learnt my lesson and afterwards I became less arrogant. My immediate need now was how to comfort my little baby who was crying a lot. She was constantly hungry and so was I; at least she had me to feed her. Incredible as it may sound in these extraordinary circumstances, I was in love with my child. So were the other mothers, even though we did not know if we would survive until the next day. We lived dreamily and completely in the present, besotted with our babies.

Maria and Nicole spent as much time as possible with me and with my daughter, whom they completely adored. We managed to organise that when I had to work at the factory one of them would stay with my baby. We all swapped shifts around and I still worked at night at Mrs. Berg's house. I saw little of George in those days. He was working long hours and when he was back he would fall asleep.

Sleeping in those days became quite a challenge; the bombing became more frequent and lasted longer. One day, when the bombing was very severe and we were in the bunker which Mrs. Berg generously shared with us, George started to draw a portrait of me on a piece of paper with coloured pencils. I do not know he had such a talent and I was very flattered. It was the eighth of February 1945. I still have this painting with the date on it. I also remember that on another day when the bombing lasted for very long time and we were in the factory bunker, George went into a state of self-pity. This brave man was holding on to my arm, his face was ashen white, and fear was in his eyes. Fear haunted us constantly and fear would break people's souls, integrity, and sanity.

But our fears were also mixed with a sense of hope; the liberation was coming, if only we could survive long enough. The Germans' fears were different. They had to worry about day-to-day survival but also they feared retaliation. Slowly the chaos becomes overwhelming. German refuges from the east were arriving, and with them stories about rape, killings and destruction arrived. They were paying the price to the winners.

Eight

One day, after a very severe raid, there was uproar in the bunker. A group of men and women returned to the camp and told us that the factory was destroyed during the bombing. George, to my relief, was among them but my friend Maria did not return. I ran into comforting arms of my beloved and was shaken by grief and crying.

"Where is Maria, what happened to her? Please dear God make her all right! Oh God, no!"

I felt such a deep desperation. Maria was not only a friend, she had become my sister. She was home, family, and comfort.

"My dear darling, I wish I could do something to make you feel better," George was trying to comfort me as best as he could. With one hand he was gently stroking my back. With the other he was just holding me tight and then he said,

"It may be a consolation to you that when the bombing started I saw her running outside. Afterwards when we could not find her, we thought that she may have escaped."

I started to calm down with the hope that she was alive and on her way to the liberated part of the west. I still called myself lucky; I had my daughter and my beloved George.

The city was burning, and it became a hell. The Germans were blowing up bridges over the River Elbe, trying to stop the enemy. Everyone in the camp was talking about the destruction of the factory and everyone agreed that it was done deliberately. Was this an act of sabotage or were the Germans trying to cover up by destroying evidence?

Many children in the camp were left without a parent and many mothers lost their children in the explosion. Also, three of the older women in our house, Stasia among them, died in this raid. My friend Boris also died under the ruins of the factory.

Each time I remember him I think about his son. When Boris died his son was only four or five years old and never would know his father. I was anxiously cuddling my daughter, worrying about what would happen to her if George and I died. Usually, she would start crying as if she understood and I had to leave these dark thoughts and smile at her. We all feared reprisal, or what would happen to us. When I asked George if he knew something about it, he refused to talk and only said

"I have no idea what could happen, and it is better if you don't ask too much about it."

This was all that I could get out of him. In those days he was silent for long periods. This would drive me to desperation and in moments like those, I doubted if he loved me and asked myself, if in other circumstances he would have been interested in me? I felt very isolated.

Since Maria's disappearance, Nicole started to be more communicative. She was helping me to look after my daughter and Juliet's violin.

One night Jan hanged himself in the same dormitory where he spent time with Juliet; he never recovered from losing her.

He was only found a few days later, after the heavy bombing stopped. Some were saying that that he sabotaged the factory in an act of revenge for Juliet's accident. No one would go to work anymore, and we all were starving. Even Mrs. Berg was losing weight. She and the Commandant were occupying one corner of the bunker.

This lunatic had a picture of Hitler on the wall as if he were God. His wife would scream at him.

"You idiot! Take this rubbish down. He took our son to his death and now he will take us."

He refused to dispose of the picture and lived with his delusion.

"You will see! This is one of our *Fuhrer's* tactics and there will be a victory for Germany."

Did he really believe it or was he completely mad? Our existence now depended on the food we could find between the raids and finding something edible in time before the next raid would start. Often the only thing we could find was a bit of fresh grass; although it was spring, not much edible was growing there. One day, George arrived back with a big sack of food. He told us that he found a half-destroyed food store and he grabbed what he could before a group of hungry Germans arrived. He told us that they were mostly women and children. For few days we had some decent food. From far we could hear shooting at the front, and we knew that soon the liberation was coming. Oh, we were waiting for so long and with such anxiety that sometimes it was painful to imagine. One day I asked George what he was planning to do once the war was over.

"We will travel to Lyon, to my parents' house. I am sure that they are fine. They will love you and our little daughter. After a holiday I will find a job. Oh, darling it will be so wonderful, you will see. We will also look for your family, I promise."

I wrinkled my forehead, considering what this all meant. It was not going back home, which is what I promised my sister. George, who noticed my apprehension, took my hands and said

"What's wrong Gala? Why are you so tense? I understand that you may worry about your family but there is nothing we can do for now, not at this moment. But once the war is over, we will talk about this again and we will work out what's the best. Stop frowning and give me a kiss." And he bent his head to kiss me, his face with a big irresistible smile. I loved him and all my doubts dissipated.

"I love you but I also love my family," I whispered weakly between kisses.

The day before liberation a group of SS men arrived and took George and another eight male prisoners with them on a truck. George quickly managed to kiss our daughter and hug me and whispered in my ear

"Go to Lyon! Please Gala! Do this! And find my parents."

He kissed me for the last time and before climbing into a truck, he turned his head and smiled at me like no one ever did. To give me courage and to let me know how much he loved me and our daughter. They drove away and we never saw them again.

Later I found out that the SS men had shot them all, accusing them of causing the factory's destruction. I was devastated but there was not much time to grieve; the survival of my daughter and me took all the time. Only in the darkness of the night my body was shaken by crying. I was feeling mutilated, the loss was irreplaceable and I was terrified by all that was happening around me. Next day the American forces arrived. With them were some black soldiers. I had never seen a black person. I felt uneasy and I pointed this to Nicole, who started to laugh. Then she said "Remember Pushkin, the Great Russian poet? He had a black grandfather and you like Pushkin, no?"

I started laughing with embarrassment at my own stupidity and ignorance and replied "Yes, I like Pushkin's writing and do not mind what colour people are, but still, I find it strange. I'm sure I will get use to the sight of black people and may find some of them very interesting."

The Americans arrested the Commandant but when they went to arrest Mrs. Berg, we all surrounded her and stopped it from happening. We told them how she treated us well and humanely and they let her go free. Before she left, she thanked us with tears in her eyes and wished us well.

Finally, we were free, but where to go? Nicole convinced me to come with her to France. I agreed only because I promised George to do so and at that time, I was not sure what I was doing.

We left the same day, taking with us small bundles of belongings. I was carrying my child, some change of clothes for my daughter and myself, and the picture of me that George drew. Nicole had a small bundle of clothes, a blanket and Juliet's violin. We walked to the west and at one point we were again involved in a raid. Now not only bombs were falling but also the allied planes shot at the ground, targeting of course the military but many civilians were also killed. During one raid we tried to take shelter in one of the bunkers, but it was overcrowded, and no one would let us in. Nicole got me into a niche inside a wall that had survived, and she pushed me down. I was holding my child under my body and Nicole was lying on top of me. The whole raid lasted for many hours, and I still don't know how we survived. Around us was such devastation and everything was burning. The extreme heat produced more heat. It was an inferno. I lost my hearing for many hours and my head was buzzing. Since that day I hear strange noises in my head that were like voices that are calling me. This always happens when I am scared.

We decided to try and find our way through the countryside, avoiding major towns, railways, or bridges. We would walk most of the time and sometimes we would get a ride with other refugees. People from all parts of Europe, were going chaotically from one place to other, often without any destination. Soon we discovered that joining others turned out to be dangerous. Two planes flew over us and started shooting at us and the other refugees. We were very lucky to survive that raid.

After this experience we left the road completely and walked through paddocks and forests. At night-time we would hide in barns or abandoned houses. These were usually ruins and probably very dangerous, but it was still very cold, especially at night. It took us many weeks to get to France. We were eating what we could find on our way; sometimes we would go into a store and demand food. Usually, the Germans would give us some bread and water and sometimes cheese, fruit, or milk. I noticed that many were happy that for them to the war was finished, and they were starting to reconstruct their lives. Their lives had been destroyed like ours, but slowly normality was starting to come back for them. Not so for us. We had in front of us an unknown road.

Once when we were crossing a forest it started to rain heavily and soon we were struggling to walk in knee-deep mud. We were lost, walking for hours in a circle, it was cold, our clothes were wet, and my little daughter was crying. We were hungry and I started to despair when Nicole pointed at something and gasped "There it is, Gala. Can you see? A house, no more than a few hundred meters away. Come, we will shelter there! Hurry or we may lose it in the darkness."

I saw a dim light in the distance; the house was hard to see. My feet were stuck in the mud and I could not move. Nicole took my daughter in her arms and with her other hand was trying to pull me out. This did not work and after a while she put everything on the ground. She opened Juliet's violin case, and gently put my daughter inside the case on top of the violin and bent to pick up a branch. She stood on steadier ground and the branch was long enough for me to reach it; slowly I managed to get out.

Soon we reached the house; build of dark heavy logs. No wonder we couldn't see it. Nicole knocked on the door and after a while the door opened. A tall woman stood there; she was an impressive figure. She was big, occupying the whole door space and was looking down at us sternly; my daughter started to cry. The woman's face softened, and she moved quickly from the door to let us in. Two small children were sitting at a table, no more than five or at the most six years old, staring at us with frightened faces. No wonder, for we must have looked like some unknown species, all covered in mud. The women said to her children

"Quickly, kids! Go and fetch me some towels from my room."

She turned towards us and with her head she pointed toward a door beside the fireplace.

"There is a laundry in this room, but it is also used as a bath. Go inside, and take your clothes off. Have a bath and I will bring you a change of clean clothes. I think that I may have some baby clothes too. Do not worry, the room is warm."

We thanked her before disappearing into the laundry. It was indeed warm. A large bath was standing by the wall behind the fireplace. I had not had a proper bath for many years. Slowly I stepped in the tub and lowered my body into the warm water. It felt heavenly. Nicole undressed my baby daughter and passed her to me. She was giggling now, happy to be warm, and soon she was sucking on my breast. I closed my eyes.

"Gala, do not fall asleep, come on, get out it is my turn now."

Laughing, Nicole was hurrying me to finish my bath. The woman came in with a pile of clothes which were much too big for us, but they were warm. And she gave me lots of clothes for my baby, saying "You can have those; my kids are grown, and I don't think that I will have more."

Shortly we were sitting around the table. The women asked us "What is your name? I am Inge and these are my children Villi and Rosie."

We told her our names. She passed us bowls of a delicious stew and, before we started eating, she said a prayer. After dinner the children played with my baby on the floor, and we helped with the washing up. Inge started to ask questions: who were we and where were we going? We told her who we were, and she spoke.

"I am so glad this war is over. It was horrible and brought so much misery to so many. My husband was a forester before the war, which is why we live here in this isolated place. He died on the front in Africa when the boy was a baby. The girl was adopted when she was a small baby, but she is now my little daughter. If anyone came to try to take her away, I would kill them. I love this girl very much. Her mother gave her to me in the market. Sometimes I think why would she do that, why? She was Jewish."

I looked at her in disbelief. Did she or did she not know what had happened in her country and the rest of Europe? I pitied her and others like her because no matter what she did or did not do, she was still German, and a load of guilt would fall on her when she found out what had happened.

I was tired and needed to sleep. My daughter fell asleep in Nicole's arms. Inge took us to a small room with a big bed and we practically collapsed. Next morning, we washed our clothes and helped Inge in her chores around the house. There was a small barn with a few hens, a pig and two goats, which Inge would milk. She also had a small patch with vegetables. We stayed with Inge for one week, until it stopped raining in a hurry and this place, lost in the forest, was safe and peaceful. Slowly I started to feel stronger. The calm and silence were like a balm. My daughter also started to calm down and she cried less. While we were waiting, Nicole started to tell us how she came to Germany before the War and ended up in Gross-Ottersleben.

Nine

Before the war Nicole lived with her grandmother in Grasse, a small town near Nice in the south of France. Her mother left her there when Nicole was five years old. She never saw her mother again. With time Nicole stopped remembering her and lived a quiet life with her grandmother. At school she learned how to read very fast, faster than the other children and showed an interest in literature. She read everything that she could get her hands on. Her grandmother did not understand her need for knowledge and insisted that she should spend more time in learning how to sew and to cook. When Nicole was turning seventeen, they started to fight a lot.

"How will you find a husband if you do not know how to cook an egg? Leave these silly books and come to help me prepare dinner. The Duvals and their son Renè are coming tonight. Yes! Yes, he is a good match, and it would be good if you showed some interest in him, perhaps you will end up better than your mother."

Nothing would irritate Nicole more than reference to her mother. She had idealised her all those years and imagined that something horrible must have happened to her mother, for otherwise why would she not come back? Her mother loved her, and Nicole would not accept any other explanation. When her grandmother mentioned her mother, she snapped and cried out.

"Leave my mother out of it! And I don't care about this stupid Renè! How can you think that I could spend all my life with such an empty person?"

Nicole ran out, shutting the door with a bang. She ran through the town's main street until she arrived at the library. Her friend

Denis was standing on a ladder putting some books away on the shelves. He turned when he heard her come in and jumped down laughing.

He took her hands and pulled her gently behind a wall, embracing her waist. Lovingly he started kissing her. Nicole began to shiver. Two months before they had started meeting in secret. Their main attraction was literature. After a long kiss Denis let go of her and spoke.

"I am leaving in a week for Germany, and I want you to come with me."

"You know that my grandmother will never give her blessing, not without us being married."

"I know! I know, but we will leave without telling her and later you can write to her and explain."

Nicole felt cold and looked at Denis, who was still smiling. What should she do? She was in love with Denis, but she also loved her grandmother who had taken care of her and was the only family she knew. Denis now stopped smiling and was looking at her with a grim expression.

When Nicole tried to come near him, he stepped backed and shouted "I thought that you loved me! But I can see! I was wrong! I dreamed of showing you Berlin and if we were lucky even meeting with Adolph Hitler."

Denis was fascinated with what was happening in Germany and believed that fascism was the answer to the failure of capitalism and communism. Nicole was not convinced and, she did not care what happened in Germany. But she did not want to disappoint Denis and agreed to go with him.

One week later they took a train to Paris and stayed in Paris for two weeks in a small hotel near the train station. It was there that Nicole lost her innocence to Denis and she was convinced that life was wonderful and she a woman with lots of luck. One night Denis arrived at the hotel with a men dressed in a black coat and a black hat. His name was Helmut. Nicole felt an instinctive dislike of him. Denis told her that they were very lucky, and that Helmut had offered to take them to Germany in his car.

He asked Nicole to pack as they were leaving immediately. Nicole spent most of the trip sleeping in the back seat. Denis and Helmut spent the trip discussing politics. Next day in the afternoon they arrived in Berlin, and they slept on the floor in the sitting room at Helmet's flat. Next day Helmut and Denis left early morning and returned very late. Nicole was annoyed for being left alone for the whole day and she told Denis so. His response was something unexpected; he raised his hand and hit her face hard in front of Helmut. Nicole fell back in shock; she felt an intense pain in her face, the pain of a broken dream like a broken mirror. Denis shouted at her.

"Never! You hear me... Never raise your voice to me! I do not like it. Now go and wash your face. We are moving to our new house."

She realised then that the love that she had dreamt of did not exist. That she had made a mistake in leaving her home. She bent her head, feeling humiliated and went to pack her bags. Shortly after, she entered her new apartment. It was fully furnished and looked as if its original owners would be back at any minute. As soon as Helmut left, Denis fell to his knees and asked her for forgiveness. Tears were rolling down his cheeks and he was saying that her pain was his.

"I do not know how I could do this. Your pain is mine. Please forgive me because I can't forgive myself! My darling! Something blinded me and I was not me."

Denis was so full of sorrow about his action that Nicole started to think that she was perhaps unjust in doubting his love. She forgave him, convinced that this incident would never be repeated. That night Denis was more passionate than ever. And for a month they had a honeymoon, and the incident was never mentioned again. Slowly Nicole cleaned the flat and discovered that it belonged to a Jewish family, the Weinbergs. They had left some clothes and letters in one cupboard and books in another.

Nicole collected these and put them in a room that she and Denis were not using. It looked as if the Weinberg had left the apartment in a hurry. One day she asked Denis if he knew where the family was. He looked at her with a glassy stare in silence. He lost the familiar velvety softness in his eyes that Nicole loved and yearned for.

"Don't know and it is not important. Perhaps they went to America. Isn't there where all the Jews go, no?" he told her.

Nicole could not say why but more and more she felt hostile towards Denis, but she was also scared of him. Denis started to go out alone and he would arrive home late at night. Nicole saw through the window that a black car would drop him, like one that Helmut had. One night Denis got home drunk, and Nicole laughingly asked him where he'd been and if he could invite her next time so she could also have some fun. First, he looked her as if he did not understand and then he hit her, more than once.

The next day he excused himself, saying that the alcohol made him lose his temper and he could not remember hitting her. That day he told her that he was working as interpreter for an important newspaper, and that he had been promoted. Nicole again forgave him. At the beginning those episodes happened every three months or so but with the start of the war the breaks were shorter.

Nicole would go out very little; she didn't speak German and Denis wanted her to stay home. She only would go out with Denis. But this was Sunday and the sun shone so she decided to walk for a while. She walked some three blocks away, where she found a small park. She remembered that Denis once took her there when things were still bearable. She found a bench and was sitting with closed eyes, enjoying the sunshine on her face, when she heard a woman's voice. She looked sideways and saw an elegantly dressed woman of middle age sitting next to her.

Nicole smiled at her and said that she didn't speak German; she got a surprise when the women responded in perfect French. Her name was Helga and she lived close by with her husband who was a journalist and was working for the same newspaper as Denis. When Nicole mentioned that Denis was working there as an interpreter, Helga looked at her in surprise but said nothing.

"Why don't you come with your husband for dinner tonight and meet Denis."

Nicole was so happy that she could speak with someone and spontaneously she invited Helga and her partner. Before leaving she gave Helga her address and again Helga was surprised.

"In the Weinberg's house?"

Nicole looked at her, not understanding what Helga was implying.

"In my house. This is where we live since we moved to Berlin and the Weinbergs went on a trip to America."

That night a surprised Denis found an elegantly dressed Nicole. She was attending to the last details to the magnificently set table for four. The table was covered by white tablecloth a vase of flowers and four candles were standing in the centre.

"And what is this celebration for? You look stunning. Who is coming?" asked Denis as he was kissing her. At that moment the doorbell rung, and Denis went to open for Helga and Rudi who had arrived with a bottle of wine. In no time the four were seated around the table and to Nicole's relief chattering in French. The conversation was around literature, art among others and Nicole was pleased that it was such successful evening. The atmosphere changed when Rudy asked Denis about his job and Denis swapped to German. Nicole understood that they were talking about the war. Before leaving Helga and Rudi extended an invitation for next Saturday.

As soon as they left Denis started to hit her and Nicole thought he was going to kill her. Denis was kicking her body and screaming at her.

"I told you not to go out! And not to talk to anyone, you bitch! You want visitors, I will bring you visitors you fuck whore!"

After he got tired of hitting her, he raped her on the floor. That night Nicole decided that she was going to leave and return home to her grandmother. Next day she found out that Germany had invaded Paris and all her plans to leave Denis seemed to disappear into nothing. They never visited Helga and Rudi. When Denis was away Nicole would run to the park and meet Helga. Once Helga saw that Nicole tried unsuccessfully to cover a bruise by her eyes with sunglasses and a scarf. Helga said nothing, only squeezed Nicole's hand and they stayed like this for a while. Before leaving Helga said "If things get very bad you can come to us, and we will help you."

And things got bad for Nicole but also for Helga. A few weeks later after their meeting in the park Helga arrived in tears at her house and begged Nicole to intervene with Denis for Rudi.

"My dear Nicole please you must help me! The Gestapo arrested Rudi because he refused to publish one of their lies in the *Volkischer Beobachter.* They are interrogating him and if they don't let him go, he will die, he suffers from a chronic heart condition."

"I would love to help you but how? Do you know something that I do not know?" Nicole asked anxiously.

"Don't tell me that you do not know about Denis?"

"Know what?"

Nicole was puzzled, not understanding what Helga was trying to say.

Finally, Helga told her "Your husband works for the Gestapo. He is translating while they are interrogating your compatriots. Nobody survives the torture."

"Are you telling me that Denis is a torturer?"

Nicole could not hear more. The truth was tremendous, and she had to think. She told Helga that she would see what she could do and sent her away. Denis didn't come back that night and next day he arrived to pack a travelling bag telling her that he was leaving for a week. He seemed happy and was singing a song meanwhile packing, he embraced and kissed Nicole. Then when he started to open her blouse, Nicole asked

"Is this true that you work for the Gestapo?"

She did not finish her question. Denis hit her and she fell across the bed, then he was on top of her and was strangling her. Nicole could not breathe and fainted. When she woke up Denis was raping her with fury. She thought that he would break her hips.

After he was satisfied, he let go of her took his bag and made a threat before leaving.

"You know I do not want you to go out? I do not want to find out what will happen if you disobey me, my love!"

During his absence Nicole packed a small bag with some clothes and hid it under the sofa. It was an unconscious act because where could she go? In Germany she knew only Helga and she was not around anymore. The war progressed; the Germans had invaded Poland and France and now Russia. Nicole was anxious as if anticipating some disaster.

Denis arrived one week later surprising her. Nicole was reading and as soon she heard the front door open, she jumped and ran into the kitchen nervously moving some pots. Denis came from behind and put something cold around her neck. Her hand touched her neck and felt her jewellery; she crumbled inside in fear with the memory still fresh off when Denis tried to strangle her. Denis kissed her on the neck and pushed her in front of a mirror. The necklace was exquisite.

Small diamante, emeralds and rubies fitted inside white gold forming small flowers with droplets of dew. Nicole saw a reflection of Denise's face in the mirror; he was looking at her intensely as if waiting for something. She forced herself to a smile and committed another mistake.

"Thank you! It is beautiful but I don't need it. It is too expensive, sell it and take me to Paris."

The fist in her face was terrifying. She started to black out, he hit her again with all his strength; she fainted and when she stopped moving, he raped her. All night he was hitting and raping her. These tortures continued until sunrise. When finally, Denis felt asleep, satisfied and snoring, she went to the bathroom naked. She took a razor and returned to the bedroom. Without blinking she cut Denis's throat. He gave a strange gurgling sound and opened his eyes for a last time. Like a fountain, blood was spilling over and soaking the bed. Nicole tossed away the knife on the bed and went to have a bath. Shortly after she dressed, took her bag from under the sofa, and carefully locked the door of the apartment, and walked to Helga's house.

She hardly recognised her. Helga looked like an old woman. Her hair had gone white, and she had an absent look and dark rings under her eyes.

"I come to tell you that Denis will not harm anyone ever again," Nicole stuttered.

Helga started laughing hysterically. "It is too late for my Rudi! And no one can hurt him, no one, ever!" and she continued laughing.

Nicole went down the street and slowly went to the train station. As if in a trance, she took the first train that was leaving and left the train when it stopped in Magdeburg. In a dream she crossed the station and walked to the street. She passed a group of women and heard one of them speak in French. Quickly she was going up to them when a soldier stopped her and spoke in German, she answered in French that she was tired; another soldier shouted something, and he left her to approach the other women. They all walked to a truck that was waiting not far away. When Nicole climbed in with the women no one ask her what she was doing there or who she was. Sometime later the trucks stopped in Grossottersleben. Juliet was carrying a violin in one hand and with the other hand she took Nicole's hand, and both entered the last house.

Inge and I were looking Nicole in silence, our mouths open in an expression of disbelief. She alone punished herself. Without knowing, she imposed a jail sentence upon herself, a sentence of four and half years. And it was not just for killing Denis or abandoning her grandmother - she also paid for the crimes that Denis had committed. I jumped up and ran to hug her.

"You don't have to punish yourself anymore! You have been punished enough and you have a right to a new beginning! It was not a crime. It was an act of justice and in your own defence."

Nicole started crying and she cried in my arms until she fell asleep. Inge spent the next day cleaning as if she wanted to avoid us and every so often, she would put her big arms around her daughter as if wanting to protect her. And every so often she cried. Two days later we left Inge's warm house.

We left her house better equipped. For start we both had rucksacks, which gave us more mobility. Now they were packed with fresh bread, cold chicken, and goat's cheese and in addition we had warm blankets. My baby had more clothes. We thanked Inge and wished her and her children well and again we were on the road.

It took us two weeks before we reached France. We ate all the food that Inge gave to us. And again, we ate what we could find on our way. As soon we reached the other side of the border, French forces picked us up and again we were arrested and taken to a camp. They interrogated us and after establishing that we were displaced people they agreed to send my daughter and myself to a refugee camp in Lyon. I convinced them on the grounds that there was a possibility that George's family was still alive and as he was the father of my child, she was French. We were given food and had a medical check-up before going to sleep in the room that was allocated to us.

Nicole was told that she was free to go home. She was in her own country, ready to pick up the pieces and start her new life. We spent this last night together talking about the future. Not mine, but Nicole's. For a change, she was the one who talked about the future and about her plans. She was going to open a boutique in the centre of Nice. I stayed silent, as I didn't know where or what my future was. I only knew that tomorrow I was travelling to Lyon and Nicole to Nice. She gave me the address of her grandmother and we promised to write to each other.

"Gala, as soon you know your address, please write to me, because even if I do not stay with my grandmother, I still will visit her and pick up your letters. Promise that you will write?"

The next morning at dawn a jeep arrived to pick up Nicole, and we fell into each other's arms and just stood there. We were overwhelmed; the past four and half years that we had spent together were more than just time; it was a lifetime that we were leaving behind. A life from which so often we had wanted to escape, and now we were terrified to let go of. I could not let go of her and was scared to be left all by myself with my baby in this strange place and with no proper knowledge of the language. My baby squeezed between us started to cry. Nicole gently opened my arms bent over to kiss my daughter and then she turned quickly and climbed into the jeep. I saw her through my tears waving her hand, the car quickly disappearing behind the first bend.

For the first time I was finally free with a small child to care for, completely on my own and with an uncertain future. As I was considering how I could get to Lyon, another jeep arrived, and a young soldier driver jumped out wearing Red Cross bands around his arms.

Once I sat in the car he smiled and asked me "We are off to Lyon, correct?"

I slowly responded in limited French - "Yes please, to Lyon."

www.ingramcontent.com/pod-product-compliance
Lightning Source LLC
LaVergne TN
LVHW010114170826
845678LV00012B/2400

* 9 7 9 8 2 2 7 1 2 5 9 4 1 *